FIXED MIX SEEKS SAME

FIXED MIX SEEKS SAME

The First Book of Dog Personal Ads

BY CHRISTINE ECKLUND
AND DEAN MINERD

**Andrews McMeel
Publishing**

Kansas City

I CHEW
You?

REBEL WITH 4 PAWS
Crate-trained Catholic schoolgirl who is a confirmed hell-raiser—muzzle that, Sister Dorothea! What you see is what you get from this straight-shooting Spaniel mix who's not afraid to jump on people or picnic tables. Know right from wrong but willing to trade risk for reward. Are you a sweet-talking, rough-neck thrill seeker who likes to throw down? Gimme a shout and come stare danger down the snout.

HAVE WE MET?
I was your randy Roman senator, your kowtown manservant in war-torn China, your lusty courtesan in sixteenth-century Venice. Ring any bells? Are we soul mates, tumbling through lifetimes together? Then come find me like always, my love, and let's see what passions we can stir this jump-and. If you're not a dog now too, let's skip it till next time.

FIXED MIX SEEKS SAME

HOT MAMMAS SERVED FRESH DAILY
Young buck eager for a mature woman to ...not getting the attention you deserve at home, come on over and we'll put those hot flashes to good use. Let's take a walk on the wild side. I'm discreet, with my own place for one-time-only or regular rendezvous.

LOSIN' MY "BOYS"
The appointment has been made. The fix is in. What I need now is one night of unbridled passion while I still have my manhood. Are you spayed? Then you know where I'm coming from. I don't care about your breed, your life story, or your favorite cheese. I just want to love you and not think about tomorrow.

BEEN AROUND THE BLOCK
The AARP Generation

A FEW MOVES LEFT
Like rap music? Me neither. Take your glucosamine tablet in a cheese cube? Me too. I want a stiff and tumble with a babe who remembers life before the Macarena and campaign-finance reform. Looks not important, but if you're a long-legged Ann-Margret type, let's smooch while I still have my teeth. No Corgis.

COUNTRY FELLER
Down-home farm boy tired to come a courtin'. If you've ever slept under the stars with a belly full of s'mores, then you know what stokes my fire. Sturdy, kind heart, good morals, and one helluva fox chaser. Lookin' to lasso a pretty little thing that knows how to rustle up a possum, likes a bath on Sunday, and doesn't mind being seen in town with a square like me.

CLEAN-LIVING DIRTY BLONDE
No-nonsense, empty-nested mother of six with great tests and teeth seeks meaningless relationship with a very naughty pup. No barkers, biters, or stupid pet tricks—been there, done that. The eye? I'll tell you all about it over dinner . . . wink, wink.

SINGLE DAD
I have one young son who is my pride and joy. He tilts my life, but there's always room for more. Legally I'm an adult—but really a kid at heart. I'm not a Don Johnson but not so bad too. I get lonely sometimes and wish that I could have someone to share my thoughts with. Your interests are none if I'm interested in you. Prefer single mom so the priorities are commonly understood. I would like to hear from you.

THE SCENT OF TRUE LOVE
Down-to-earth Bloodhound with a nose for bull. Had a near-death experience when I choked on a biscuit. Now I'd rather watch the ...and knows how to make a huntin' dog's jowls drop. If you like the simple life, there's room for two on my front porch. Bichon Frises? I reckon not.

WHO'S YOUR DADDY?
I've had enough of old broads trying to teach me new tricks. Now I want 'em young and stupid. If you haven't even broken in your first squeeze toy and don't understand "sit" yet, then maybe we can play. Just be paper trained.

MULLET UNDER CONSTRUCTION
Recently out lesbian bitch looking to get my feet wet in the waters of Sapphic sisterhood. I enjoy lumberyards, HGTV, sunsets, and anything from Eva Cassidy. You be figure, gentle and understanding of an old dog on a new path. Looking forward to sharing the rainbow of my orgasm with someone other than myself. Kate Couric look-alikes a real +.

BLUE-COLLAR CASTLE
Doublewide King ready to crown my new Queen. Honest-living, honest-loving tow-truck assist wants someone to share the good times with. Got 2 kids that live with their mother in Prescott. Not looking for more. Full-figure gals make me smile. Writing ain't my thing, so if you like what you see and have all your teeth, then hit me up and we'll take it from there.

IT'S NEVER TOO LATE
Long-in-the-tooth tramp type looking for a Lady to love. Seen the U.S. of A. from the cab of an 18-wheeler. Had the good fortune to pee in 43 different states, with pictures to prove it. Now lookin' to put down some roots and proper-scoop my own backyard. Ready for this: picket fence, home-cooked meals, and a litter to teach how to play ball. Stable provider with benefits and enough savings to stake out future. Will you be part of it?

SUPER SENIOR
Former stray seeks soul mate to spend twilight with. Friends first and then . . . ? Cataracts have given me the chance to look inside, and I like what I see. Are you what else I'm looking for? Abusers and neglecters move on. This old-timer's seen it all. Surprise me.

HAVE YOU SEEN MY HEART?
Recently ended a long-term relationship or, rather, it ended me. I'm giving love one last try before I bury my heart for good. I don't help the blind cross the street or save small dogs from burning buildings. I'm just a dog asking another dog to love me. Interested? Then start digging.

I'VE GOT ONE LEFT AFTER MY DIVORCE

This book is dedicated to the memory of our friend Julie Hayden. As a goofy animal lover and dedicated rescuer, she saved a lot of dogs' lives. The least we can do now is get them dates.

EBONY PRINCESS

Waiting for her king. My girlfriends say my standards are too high. You should see the mutts they date. You are: strong, intelligent, generous, sexy, clean, funny, unattached. I am: ready. I've had my share of squeak toys. Where's my man? Respond with plans. P.S.: I love massage.

CHUB WANTS TO BE CHASED

Middle-aged, plus-sized playmate voracious for boy bands and all smoked meats. Will let the right man catch me. If you like what you see and can handle tons of fun, then give this passionate and appreciative lover what she's hungering for. This yo-yo dieter is love starved!

GIVE ME A "TRY"

Pretty pup squad leader seeks handsome jock or other athletic muscleman for sideline skirmishes. Do you have what it takes to give this good-time girl something to really cheer about? Open to all passes and ready to tackle a monogamous relationship if we're both on the same playing field. Let's hit the showers and see if we can take it into overtime.

ECHO PARK ARTIST SEEKS MUSE

Bohemian sculptress looking to create future with a model of goddess proportions. If you know the true Zen meaning of the word "sit," then your inspiration is all I'm lacking to truly soar. Work in progress with a passion for all things lovely. Confidence is sexy—not flaunting it is sexier. If you're an organic vegan, there's no limit to the artistry of our girl-on-girl love thang.

FASHION POLICE DOG

Get a "cute" turtleneck for Christmas? Maybe a plaid jacket with snaps and a matching beret? How about those "adorable" quilted antlers everyone thinks are so sweet on a dog? Sound like you? Then go find yourself a Poodle. On the other hand, if you share my eye for progressive style and my nose for the avant-garde, then maybe I'll give you a sniff. I said *maybe*.

COLD PAWS – WARM HEART

X-treme sports femme in touch with my inner wolf. If that's wack to you, then you better bail now. Ever heard the call of the wild and didn't let it go to voice mail? Then I bet we'll connect. Saint Bernards and other fresh-powder buds are hella rad. Let's pee our names in the snow! I'm stoked!

ISLAND LEI

Pineapple heiress on a mainland manhunt. My arranged marriage was annulled and I'm free to find the broad-shouldered military (or ex-military) hero of my dreams. I'm a sucker for a Shepherd in dog tags! If you've got a

VOODOO PRIESTESS

N'Orleans madam with a penchant for other Pugs and a taste for black magic. Aquarian, Stevie Nicks fan who's on the cusp of something truly divine. If you're a Virgo whose moon is rising, then our ultimate destiny may be falling in love. I've tried spells, talismans, and chicken-bone altars to find you. (Okay, the chicken was a snack, but you get the picture.) Is our harmonic convergence in the cards? Don't let's fight fate.

SINGLE RIDER TO SHARE A CAB AND MORE

Dynamic and fun Upper East Side girl enjoys spa days, dinners out, shopping, and only chews Manolos. Loves Bryant Park on summer nights, cold sesame noodles and the *Times* in bed on Sundays. Can you get my friends to like you without having to flirt with them? My meter's running, so let's have Snacks in the City.

FIRST CLASS NOW BOARDING

Let's travel the world together and leave our emotional baggage at home. Wash-and-go globetrotter who wants to check my inhibitions and carry on with an international playmate. Member of the mile-high club who will only consider "doodie-free" frequent fliers. Fasten your seat belt. I'm your passport to adventure.

RESCUE MY HEART

Former pound pup wants to share new leash on life with free-spirited height-and-weight proportionate soul mate. Let's duet "Unchained Melody" as we ride with our heads out the car window. Just had my teeth cleaned. Mange is long gone but I've got another itch to scratch. I'm not afraid to get my fur matted, so let's have fun, fun, fun!

IT'S MY TURN

Stardom is in my blood. My grandmother did *Johnny Carson* twice with Joan Embry. My mother booked a guest shot on *21 Jump Street*. They say my father did some stunt work on *Baywatch* but I never knew him (long story). I am: gorgeous, scary talented, ambitious, and unstoppable. You are: connected, not threatened, able to chew with your mouth closed. No musicians, actors, or nonguild writers. Producers and directors move to the head of the line.

MALES
Alpha Dogs

PARTY AT MY HOUSE!

Yo! Yo! Yo! What up, senoritas?! The family is gone and the crib is mine! So let's howl at the moon and roll around on the new carpet. Bring your housebroken, fixed friends, and

---

can eat to the one who can get the refrigerator open. Peace out, y'all! Aaigght?

MURRAY THE K-9

Orthodox mensch who's tired of shvitzing over finding the perfect Jewish-American Poodle. Willing to reform my love life for the right family-oriented shiksa with broad, childbearing hips. I'll walk away from the chuppah and the hoopla if you are my chosen one. I'm the dreamboat that your mother wants you to marry—what are you waiting for? This schlemiel is ready to make a deal.

MR. NICE GUY

Old enough to shave, but still a boy at heart. All my women friends say I'm too great a catch to be single. What gives? Good manners and strong values make for lonely Saturday nights. Nice feeling (says my mom), polite, and obedient. Is there a girl out there who wants a traditional guy who still believes in ladies first and the magic of a first sniff? Thank you for your consideration.

DISTEMPERAMENTAL, BUT WORTH IT

No more meds, no more shrinks. I say love me, love my Gemini mood swings. One day I'm sniffing the pretty daisies, and the next I'm gnawing on the remote control, wishing it would ram. Needless to say, I'm an excellent kisser. So look me up, but you probably won't. I hate you. I like classical music. How about you?

2 FAST 2 FURRY

Want to ride shotgun as we cruise down the boulevard of true love? Low-riding, street-smart hombre with four on the floor seeks fast women for high-octane adventures. Let me pop under your hood and make your engine purr. If you know how to check a dipstick and look good in cha-cha pants, then let's give it a test drive.

COCKEYED OPTIMIST

I still believe in love at first sight, sleeping at the foot of the bed, and "heel." I love how I smell after a bath but can't wait to roll in the mud. A nap in the sun, a scratch behind the ear, and an occasional leg hump are what keep me chasing my tail. I think dog shows should be outlawed, cats are for chasing and doggie day care is for wimps. Let me know if we see eye to eye.

PURE MUSCLE

All-natural bodybuilder who likes to pump it up with other buff muscle dudes is looking to be worshipped by worked-out hunks. Very butch— 11 pounds of solid muscle—8% body fat—6-pack abs—big guns—trimmed body hair—nice bubble butt. My pic is for real—you should be too. Will be in Tucson for Pride weekend. Show me what you got, boy! Let's party and play!

... very, very sleepy ... look deep, deep into
my eyes, Miss Sagittarius ... let go ... yes ...
do not resist ... you are mine ... yes ...
come to me ... yes ... bring us a snack ...
that's it ... that's it ... sit ... stay ... yes ...
good girl ...

YOU HAD ME AT ROLL OVER

Top Dog, Tom Cruise look-alike, seeks sassy
Penelope Cruz-ish Chihuahua to pull theat
G's with. If you dig Jerky McGuire, doing Risky
Business, and don't think that love is a
Mission Impossible, then I'm the Cocktail
Wiener dog for you. Do you have what it takes
to be my leading lady? Let's jump on the
casting couch and find out.

FIVE THINGS I CAN'T LIVE WITHOUT

Broken-in Tennis Balls. Peanut Butter. Public
Television. Love. Broken-in Tennis Balls.

GOING MY WAY?

Forward-thinking bon vivant with an eye
toward where I've been. Willing to trade my
soul for a 9-pack of chicken tenders and a
Shiatsu massage. Well traveled, overeducated, lighthearted. Is it true I'm single because
I keep looking for a Bond girl in a dive bar?
True love and objects in mirror are closer
than they appear. I'd rather be at the Hilton
in Paris than with Paris Hilton. Life's a trip—
pack lightly. Give me a call and start breaking my heart.

KNOCK KNOCK

Funnyman cutup is seriously looking for you.
My comedy may be stand-up, but I'll take my
love lyin' down. If fart jokes make you howl
and you see the upside of short ribs, then
what are we waiting for? When I tell you you
have a beautiful body, will you hold it against
me? Let's redefine the whoopee cushion.

SCOOBY DO ME

Sex K-urban hipster digs Kristos in the park
statue, cartoons, and all things random.
Spiritual, not religious — Spinoza, Deepak
Kabbalah. For a philosophy buff with pick-up
freelance Seeing Eye skills for extra cash. If
you're looking for answers you aren't afraid to
chase it for a couple of years. Let's fetch a
couple of chai lattes and see if we connect.
The muzzle's just some bling bling, so let's do
art.

DIGNITY?

They dress me in a tutu and make me twirl
for their treats. I've been the Easter Bunny, a
scarecrow, a reindeer (see above), a leprechaun and a diapered cupid. I had no
choice. They were feeding me. Who would you
trust me if you said ...

"DOG" SPELLED BACKWARDS

Mr. Sexy. Irresistible. Brilliant. Scorpio.
Insatiable. Hot. SEXY. God.

...analyst says ... his obsessive-compulsive
goose down has kept me single too long—a
complicated saga that I look forward to sharing. Obsessive-compulsive with all my biscuits in a row. Bald patches are filling in
nicely and my involuntary paw-washing is in
check. Let's get ready to love.

CONTENTS

INTRODUCTION ix

FEMALES 1
Looking for Mr. Goodbone

MALES 21
Alpha Dogs

PUPPY LOVE 41
Still Going on the Paper

BEEN AROUND THE BLOCK 51
The AARF Generation

ANYTHING GOES 65
Dogs Gone Wild

CHANCE MEETINGS 79
Waiting to Go Out

I'M A CLICHÉ

I stick my head out the car window. I sniff
fire hydrants, cut grass, and have an eclectic
collection of roadside finery. I sleep with my
head between the couch cushions, and get a
cup of yummy ice-cream every time for my
birthday. No apologies, no regrets. I'm a dog
doing my job, looking for a bitch who appreciates my handiwork.

CELIBATE AND FETCHING

I was a sex addict: I mean I fetch. Big sticks,
small sticks, birch, pine, oak, table legs,
24/7. I do get pissy for a lady. Just because
I'm on a diet doesn't mean I can't look at the
menu ... If a nice guy working through his
sexual issues sounds like your cup of tea,
then let's bring home some lumber together.

LAST CALL

My trust fund has run out. The party has
moved on. Reformed Lothario, hard-headed
Jack Russell finally ready to settle down by a
warm fire for long evenings of wine, jazz and

...past? If you're old and ugly, please be rich.

PUPPY LOVE
Still Going on the Paper

NEW YORK NOOKIE

I think backyards are for sissies? Do you get
off on humans picking up after you with
those little plastic bags? (It's the law?) If
you're a bitch who loves the smell of day-old
weenie water, midtown hydrants, and a nice
summer garbage strike, then let's hook up
and do Gotham doggy style. You got a problem with that??

DON'T TELL MY DADDY

Barely legal freshman who's looking for an
education in love. Boys at home were all
thumbs — I need a sophisticated city fella to
show me the finer points of romance. Are you
generous enough to share your experience
with this petite and insatiable coed? Little
thing like me could get lost in this expensive
town without a big strong escort. Professional
gents only please—married men encouraged.

HE'S NEVER WRONG

My imaginary friend had a dream about you
last night. You had a silky coat and a sexy
bark. You ate grass and liver and hated
gunfights on TV and having your teeth
cleaned. You loved cheese, pepperoni sticks,
and especially me. Are you too good to be
true? Fine with me. That's what imaginary
friends are for—to tell you outrageous
gentleness.

I CHEW

You?

REBEL WITH 4 PAWS

Crate-trained Cairn-ies, scrappier who's a
reformed hell-raiser ... inside out. Sicko-
Doubtout! What you see is what you get from
this straight-shooting Spanish mix chips not
afraid to jump on people or pitch an Editor.
Know right from wrong but willing to trash
out for reward. Are you a closet-taking
rough neck that seeks who has to think
down? Gimme a shout and come stare danger down the snout.

HAVE WE MET?

I was your randy Roman senator, your lovelorn
manservant in war-torn China, your lusty
courtesan in sixteenth-century Venice. Ring
any bells? Are we soul-mates, tumbling
through lifetimes together? Been there but
I'm the already. My eyes and art lives and
pancreas we can on this romance. If you're
not a dog now too, let's skip a bit part here.

HOT MAMAS SERVED FRESH DAILY

PURE MUSCLE

All-natural bodybuilder who likes to pump it up with other buff muscle dudes is looking to be worshipped by worked-out hunks. Very butch—11 pounds of solid muscle—8% body fat—6-pack abs—big guns—trimmed body hair—nice bubble butt. My pic is for real—you should be too. Will be in Tucson for Pride weekend. Show me what you got, boy! Let's party and play!

YOU ARE GETTING SLEEPY . . .

. . . very, very sleepy . . . look deep, deep into my eyes, Miss Sagittarius . . . let go . . . yes . . . do not resist . . . you are mine . . . yes . . . come to me . . . yes . . . bring us a snack . . . that's it . . . that's it . . . sit . . . stay . . . yes . . . good girl . . .

YOU HAD ME AT ROLL OVER

Top Dog, Tom Cruise look-alike, seeks sassy Penelope Cruz-ish Chihuahua to pull three G's with. If you dig Jerky Maguire, doing Risky Business, and don't think that love is a Mission Impossible, then I'm the Cocktail Wiener dog for you. Do you have what it takes to be my leading lady? Let's jump on the casting couch and find out.

FIVE THINGS I CAN'T LIVE WITHOUT

Broken-in Tennis Balls. Peanut Butter. Public Television. Love. Broken-in Tennis Balls.

GOING MY WAY?

Forward-thinking bon vivant with an eye toward where I've been. Willing to trade my soul for a 9-pack of chicken tenders and a Shiatsu massage. Well traveled: overeducated, lighthearted. Is it true I'm single because I keep looking for a Bond girl in a dive bar? True love and objects in mirror are closer than they appear. I'd rather be at the Hilton in Paris than with Paris Hilton. Life's a trip—pack lightly. Give me a call and start breaking my heart.

KNOCK KNOCK

Funnyman cutup is seriously looking for you. My comedy may be stand-up, but I'll take my love lyin' down. If fart jokes make you howl and you see the upside of short men, then what are we waiting for? When I tell you you have a beautiful body, will you hold it against me?! Let's redefine the whoopee cushion.

SCOOBY DO ME

Gen X, urban hipster digs Frisbee in the park, classic cartoons, and all things random. Spiritual, not religious—Spinoza, Deepak Kabbalah. I'm a philosophy buff who picks up freelance Seeing Eye shifts for extra cash. If you're looking for nirvana and aren't afraid to chase it for a couple of blocks, let's fetch a couple of chai lattes and see if we connect. The muzzle's just some bling bling, so let's do it!

. . . for liver treats. I've been the Easter bunny, a scarecrow, a reindeer (see above), a leprechaun, and a diapered cupid. I had no choice. They were feeding me. Why should you date me? If not you, who?

"DOG" SPELLED BACKWARDS

ME: Sexy. Irresistible. Brilliant. Scorpio. Insatiable. Hot. SEXY. God.
YOU: Lucky.

MIXED NUT

My analyst says I'm cured. Irrational fear of goose down has kept me single too long—a complicated saga that I look forward to sharing. Obsessive-compulsive with all my biscuits in a row. Bald patches are filling in nicely and my involuntary paw-washing is in check. Let's get crazy in love.

I'M A CLICHÉ

I stick my head out the car window. I sniff tree trunks, eat grass, and have an eclectic collection of rawhide bonery. I sleep with my head between the couch cushions, and get a cup of vanilla ice cream every year for my birthday. No apologies, no regrets. I'm a dog doing my job, looking for a pooch who appreciates my handiwork.

CELIBATE AND FETCHING

I was a sex addict, now I fetch. Big sticks, small sticks, birch, pine, oak, table legs, 24/7. I do get lonely for a lady. (Just because I'm on a diet doesn't mean I can't look at the menu . . .) If a nice guy working through his sexual issues sounds like your cup of tea, then let's bring home some lumber together.

LAST CALL

My trust fund has run out. The party has moved on. Reformed Lothario, toilet-breathed Jack Russell finally ready to settle down by a warm fire for long evenings of pigs ears and Pictionary. Are you the lady who can help me forget the bodacious pups of my mad-dog past? If you're old and ugly, please be rich.

PUPPY LOVE
Still Going on the Paper

NEW YORK NOOKIE

Think backyards are for sissies? Do you get off on humans picking up after you with those little plastic bags? (It's the law!) If you're a bitch who loves the smell of day-old weenie water, midtown hydrants, and a nice summer garbage strike, then let's hook up and do Gotham doggy style. You got a problem with that??

DON'T TELL MY DADDY

Barely legal freshman who's looking for an education in love. Boys at home were all

---

. . . generous enough to share your experience with this petite and insatiable coed? Little thing like me could get lost in this expensive town without a big, strong escort. Professional gents only, please—married men encouraged.

HE'S NEVER WRONG

My imaginary friend had a dream about you last night. You had a silky coat, and a sexy bark. You ate grass and liver, and hated gunfights on TV, and having your teeth cleaned. You loved cheese, pepperoni sticks and especially me. Are you too good to be true? Fine with me. That's what imaginary friends are for—to find you imaginary girlfriends.

I CHEW

You?

REBEL WITH 4 PAWS

Crate-trained Catholic schoolgirl who is a confirmed hell-raiser—muzzle that, Sister Dorothea! What you see is what you get from this straight-shooting Spaniel mix who's not afraid to jump on people or picnic tables. Know right from wrong but willing to trade risk for reward. Are you a sweet-talking, tough-neck thrill seeker who likes to throw down? Gimme a shout and come stare danger down the snout.

HAVE WE MET?

I was your randy Roman senator, your lovelorn manservant in war-torn China, your lusty courtesan in sixteenth-century Venice. Ring any bells? Are we soul mates, tumbling through lifetimes together? Then come find me like always, my love, and let's see what passions we can stir this go-round. If you're not a dog now too, let's skip it till next time.

HOT MAMAS SERVED FRESH DAILY

Young buck eager to show a mature woman to show him the ropes. I'm all ears when it comes to what you have to teach me. If you're not getting the attention you deserve at home, come on over and we'll put those hot flashes to good use. Let's take a walk on the wild side. I'm discreet, with my own place for one-time-only or regular rendezvous.

LOSIN' MY "BOYS"

The appointment has been made. The fix is in. What I need now is one night of unneutered passion while I still have my manhood. Are you spayed? Then you know where I'm coming from. I don't care about your breed, your life story, or your favorite cheese. I just want to love you and not think about tomorrow.

BEEN AROUND THE BLOCK
The AARF Generation

...dog music. Me fetches, cake your glucosamine tablet in a cheese cube? Me too. I
want a sniff and tumble with a babe who
remembers life before the Macarena and
campaign-finance reform. Looks not important, but if you're a long-legged Ann-Margret
type, let's smooch while I still have my teeth.
No Corgis.

COUNTRY FELLER

Down-home farm boy from 'In' come a-
courtin'. If you've ever slept under the stars
with a belly full of s'mores, then you know
what shakes my fur. Sturdy, kind heart, good
morals, and one helluva fur chaser. Lookin' to
lasso a pretty little thing that knows how to
rustle up a possum, takes a bath on Sunday,
and doesn't mind being seen in town with a
square like me.

CLEAN-LIVING DIRTY BLONDE

No-nonsense, empty-nested mother of six
with great teeth and fresh seeks meaningless
relationship with a very naughty boy. No
barkers, biters, or stupid pet tricks—been
there, done that. The eye? I'll tell you all
about it over dinner ... wink, wink.

SINGLE DAD

I have one young son who is my pride and joy.
He fills my life, but there's always room for
more. Legally I'm an adult—but really a kid
at heart. I'm not a Dad Johnson but not so
bad too. I get lonely sometimes and wish that
I could have someone to share my thoughts
with. Your interests are mine if I'm interested
in you. Prefer single mom so the pooches are
community important. I would like to hear
from you.

THE SCENT OF TRUE LOVE

Down-to-earth Bloodhound with a nose for
golf. Not a neat-freak, especially when it
comes to slobber. You'd rather spend the
night in than out. Tired of the hair of a
new romance? Prefer who is loving, low-key,
and knows how to make a hound' dog's spirits
drop. If you like the simple life, there's room
for two on a front porch. Bichon Frises? I
throw up.

WHO'S YOUR DADDY?

I've had enough of old bitch trying to teach
me tricks to do. Don't need 'em young and
dumb to entertain me when it comes down to
real bidness I'm what she's aimin' for. The
girl that makes us one play hard for papa
Lonnie.

MULLET UNDER CONSTRUCTION

[illegible text continues]

[second column]

myself. Katie Couric look-alikes a real +.

BLUE-COLLAR CASTLE

Doubleblade King ready to crown my new
Queen. Honest-living, honest-loving tow-truck
assist wants someone to share the good
times with. Our 2 kids that live with their
mother in Prescott. Not looking for more. Full-
figure girls make me smile. Writing isn't my
thing, so if you like what you see and want all
your teeth, then hit me up and we'll take it
from there.

IT'S NEVER TOO LATE

Long-in-the-tooth tramp type looking for a
lady to love. Seen the U.S. at A, from tip-cab
of an 18-wheeler. Had the good fortune to pee
in 43 different states, with pictures to prove
it. Now lookin' to put down some roots and
pooper-scoop my own backyard. Ready for the
picket fence, home-cooked meals and a little
to teach how to play ball. Stable provider—
full benefits and enough savings to stake our
future. Will you be part of it?

SUPER SENIOR

Former stray seeks soul mate to spend twilight with. Friendly first, and then...
Cataracts have given me the chance to look
inside, and I like what I see. Are you what
else I'm looking for? Abusers and bogbullers
move on. This old-timer's spent it all. 'Suppose
me.

HAVE YOU SEEN MY HEART?

Recently ended a long-term relationship or,
rather, it ended me. I'm giving love another
try before I bury my heart for good. I don't
help the blood cross the street to save our
deer from furious floodings. I'm just a dog
asking another dog to love me. Interested?
Then start digging.

I'VE GOT ONE LEFT AFTER MY DIVORCE

Recently single and a risk to everyone. Got
bitten—and once. A damsel with her front-
bone on her tennis is bound to alive ... especially when your overlooking half-broken kids
with any. If I can unwind a name that's helped to
overtake and am unstucy there, I'm ... playing
dog-seeks comering, no-stiff chonces who
wishes steal has spirits.

ANYTHING GOES

Dogs bark, bark.

RETIRED LORD AND LADY SEEK WILLING PEASANTS

Our children are grown and we're ready to
crown the Duke and Duchess of our castle.
Breeders seek well-mannered assist to help
us with daily chores. Pure-bred subjects, but
Discreet, not of royal blood, and withwatch
submissive. Sound like Camelot? Then let's
meet at the next jousting fair, and only the
[illegible text continues]

[third column]

INTRODUCTION

Fixed Mix Seeks Same was
spawned one morning when
Dean was offering his daily
dose of encouragement to his
beloved mixed breed, Scout
(see: *Ever Been Kissed by a
Scorpio?*). He reminded her
that she was really quite
something with her shapely
medium size, taut hind end,
and typical Scorpio can-do
attitude. It sounded so much
like a personal ad that Dean
wrote it out and e-mailed it to
his equally dog-nutty writer
friend Christine. She immedi-
ately volleyed back with an ad
for her pride and joy, Phil (see:
Last Call), the toilet-breathed
Jack Russell who yearns for
romantic nights of pig's ears
and Pictionary. Many tears of
laughter later, *Fixed Mix Seeks
Same* was born.

   Fixed Mix Seeks Same cele-
brates dogs, love, and all the
comedy therein.

ONE LUMP OR TWO?

[illegible text]

YES, LADIES, WE'RE SINGLE

[illegible text]

like rap music! Me neither. Take your glucosamine tablet in a cheese cube? Me too. I
want a sniff and tumble with a babe who
remembers life before the Macarena and
campaign-finance reform. Looks not important, but if you're a long-legged Ann-Margret
type, let's smooch while I still have my teeth.
No Corgis.

COUNTRY FELLER
Down-home farm boy fixin' to come a-
courtin'. If you've ever slept under the stars
with a belly full of s'mores, then you know
what stokes my fire. Sturdy, kind heart, good
morals, and one helluva fox chaser. Lookin' to
lasso a pretty little thing that knows how to
rustle up a possum, likes a bath on Sunday,
and doesn't mind being seen in town with a
square like me.

CLEAN-LIVING DIRTY BLONDE
No-nonsense, empty-nested mother of six
with great teeth and teeth seeks meaningless
relationship with a very naughty boy. No
barkers, biters, or stupid pet tricks—been
there, done that. The eye? I'll tell you all
about it over dinner . . . wink, wink.

SINGLE DAD
I have one young son who is my pride and joy.
He fills my life, but there's always room for
more. Legally I'm an adult—but really a kid
at heart. I'm not a Don Johnson but not so
bad too. I get lonely sometimes and wish that
I could have someone to share my thoughts
with. Your interests are mine if I'm interested
in you. Prefer single mom so the priorities are
commonly understood. I would like to hear
from you.

THE SCENT OF TRUE LOVE
Down-to-earth Bloodhound with a nose for
bull. Had a near-death experience when I
choked on a biscuit. Now I'd rather watch the
squirrels than chase them. On the trail of a
new romantic partner who is loving, licensed,
and knows how to make a huntin' dog's jowls
drop. If you like the simple life, there's room
for two on my front porch. Bichon Frises? I
reckon not.

WHO'S YOUR DADDY?
I've had enough of old broads trying to teach
me new tricks. Now I want 'em young and
stupid. If you haven't even broken in your
first squeaky toy and don't understand "no"
yet, then maybe we can play. Just be paper
trained.

MULLET UNDER CONSTRUCTION
Recently out lesbian mom looking to get my
feet wet in the waters of Sappho sisterhood. I
enjoy lumberyards, HGTV, sunsets, and anything from Eva Cassidy. To be lipstick, gentle, and understanding of an old dog on a new
oath. Looking forward to sharing the rainbow

---

myself. Katie Couric look-alikes a real +.

BLUE-COLLAR CASTLE
Doublewide King ready to crown my new
Queen. Honest-living, honest-loving tow-truck
assist wants someone to share the good
times with. Got 2 kids that live with their
mother in Prescott. Not looking for more. Full-
figure girls make me smile. Writing ain't my
thing, so if you like what you see and have all
your teeth, then hit me up and we'll take it
from there.

IT'S NEVER TOO LATE
Long-in-the-tooth Tramp type looking for a
Lady to love. Seen the U.S. of A. from the cab
of an 18-wheeler. Had the good fortune to pee
in 43 different states, with pictures to prove
it. Now lookin' to put down some roots and
pooper-scoop my own backyard. Ready for the
picket fence, home-cooked meals, and a litter
to teach how to play ball. Stable provider—
full benefits and enough savings to stake our
future. Will you be part of it?

SUPER SENIOR
Former stray seeks soul mate to spend twilight with. Friends first and then . . . ?
Cataracts have given me the chance to look
inside, and I like what I see. Are you what
else I'm looking for? Abusers and neglecters
move on. This old-timer's seen it all. Surprise
me.

HAVE YOU SEEN MY HEART?
Recently ended a long-term relationship or,
rather, it ended me. I'm giving love one last
try before I bury my heart for good. I don't
help the blind cross the street or save children from burning buildings. I'm just a dog
asking another dog to love me. Interested?
Then start digging.

I'VE GOT ONE LEFT AFTER MY DIVORCE
Recently single and back in circulation. Not
bitter—just wiser. A woman with too much
time on her hands is bound to stray—especially when your freeloading half brother lives
with you. I've cleaned house (God forbid she
ever did) and am ready to move on. Cheating,
lying, selfish, controlling, vindictive ballbusters need not apply.

ANYTHING GOES
Dogs Gone Wild

RETIRED LORD AND LADY SEEK WILLING
PEASANTS
The children are grown and we're ready to
lower the drawbridge and have some
medieval fun with a like-minded couple. Us:
Naughty infidels, not easy to shock. You:
Discreet, not of royal blood, and extremely
submissive. Sound like Camelot? Then let's
meet at the renaissance fair, and ride the

ONE LUMP OR TWO?
Territorial Teacup with S&M bent demands
submissive playthings for long nights of
pleasure and pain. My nails are clipped but
not my libido. If you've been a bad, bad boy,
then I want to hear from you. Are you man
enough to be my lapdog? I thought so. Roll
over and beg.

YES, LADIES, WE'RE SINGLE
Two fun L.A. brothers (adopted) seek two
extraordinary Poodlettes (same litter okay) for
indoor/outdoor games. All you need to know is
we're bathed, neutered, and very limber.
Come love the fairy tail. What happens in
Silver Lake, stays in Silver Lake.

I LIKE TO DRESS UP
Plucky mutt who looks great in heels. I've
been Marilyn for Halloween, Barbra on my
birthday, and Boy George for the hell of it. I'm
looking for a sensitive sidekick who shares
my love of all things costume. Breed not
important, but if you're good with a needle
and thread so much the better. No fleas. No
queens. No kidding.

I'M NOT AS CRAZY AS I LOOK—I'M CRAZIER
Petite and powerful Natalie Wood type who
can swim. Shiny brindle coat, hypnotic eyes,
full lips, and a fire down below! No-limits
party girl who digs a good dig and respects a
man who knows how to bury a bone. Let's
hook up if you wanna push my envelope and
nip at the mailman of passion.

OPEN RELATIONSHIP
She's bi-curious with a taut, hot body that is
one raw nerve I can't seem to satisfy alone. I
like to share, love to watch, and will let you
walk away with all photo negatives. You be
tartar free and eager to please. Droolers
encouraged. The rest is chemistry.

ON THE LAM FROM ANIMAL CONTROL
Maybe I did bite the UPS man. I can't be the
only one who hates that brown uniform. I'm
incognito, on the run, and I could sure use a
little love and a good meal. If you like bad
boys and have a nice doghouse-for-two away
from the glaring eye of the law, then maybe
you're what I'm looking for. No hang-ups
please. I have my own problems.

FOUR LEGS OVER EASY
Gourmet girl with few limits wants men with
big appetites and enormous spatulas to tip
me over for an all-you-can-eat buffet. Sloppy
eaters at my house make for a feast on the
floor. First come, first served. If you like it hot
and spicy and know your way around the
kitchen, then let's get cooking. Seconds anyone?

Petite Latina needs a new place to live, they threw me out. Excuse me if I have a small bladder and no impulse control. I can't think romance right now, but once I settle into your place, who knows. Only respond if you don't have any carpet. I've been through enough. And no Boxers. I'm not *that* desperate.

DON'T JUDGE WHAT YOU DON'T UNDERSTAND

Mixed couple with no limits and no tolerance for prejudice. We seek other open singles and couples who see past the societal barriers and into the true meaning of love. We host free, bi-monthly swing events at our San Fernando Valley home. Leave your inhibitions at the door. The hot tub is ready—snacks and towels provided. All welcome—single men must be prescreened. Peace.

ROLE-PLAY FANTASIES EXPLORED

Creative, open-minded Beagle invites dominant females for massage, body worship, and bondage games at my private Pasadena doghouse. Let's play Veterinarian, Postman, or Spin the Rawhide. Please be imaginative, verbal, and flexible. I can take a lickin' and give one too. Short-hair breed preferred—but won't discriminate. Your pleasure is my only goal, Mistress

IGNORE MY WIFE

Sorry you ever shed singlehood? Me too. Need to break free from the choke chain of relentless "companionship" and commitment? Ditto. Sick of the barked orders, the whimpering guilt trips, the honey-do list? I hear you. Enough is finally enough. Let's walk out our doggy doors and into each other's heart. You first.

CHANCE MEETINGS
Waiting to Go Out

LONE PINE CAMPGROUND: LAST FOURTH OF JULY

You're black, on the right. We hid behind some rock and sat out the fireworks. We shared bite shakes... and more, but no one found familiar? Well, you're a father, but I have four daughters and a son who want to meet their daddy. Come home. Yes, of course they're yours.

YOGAWORKS ON MAIN

Dynamo. Last Thursday morning. I complimented the arch on your Downward Facing Dog. You thought my Cat Pose was aligned in... I've recently shed my negative karma chain... shared experiences, forced obedience... quickly... my loyalty ready to shower... energy. If not we'll the vibe too then lets start Together. Namaste

WHERE ARE YOU?

...back to health, I enrolled you in insulin because I thought we were falling in love. You promised you'd come back and take me away from my evil parents who never let me do anything. It's been two months. Where the @#$%&* are you? I'm going nuts here. No questions asked.

RIVERSIDE DOG PARK

We run for the ball and Frisbee, and carried it back together. So began the three most glorious days of my life. We fetched, we laughed, we loved. We both liked beef strips, and hated the same Pomeranian. I thought we had something. Then you stopped playing. I ran away, trying to find you. Now I'm leashed, and lonely, and I can't look at a Frisbee without crying. Come back. I'll wait.

DR. CONDELLO'S MANGE CLINIC

We both looked prehistoric, and had some good laughs between scratches. I've cleaned up since then, and am having a hard time finding a guy who wants me for more than my great looks. Just wanted to reconnect with someone who seemed to get me. Sure hope you've cleared up too. If not, that's cool. You have nice eyes.

NORTH SHORE ANIMAL SHELTER

We heard you escaped! Remember us, Bro? Before the shelter we all ran like wolves together, free, living out of Dumpsters, a tight pack. Look at us now. Man! We're clean, living in fancy houses, and have an expensive dog walker. Are you back on the street? Still "Sparkley"? If it's time to come in from the cold, Dode. Let's get the old posse together and pick through some high-falutin trash! C'mon Dawg!

...BY A SCORPIO?

Medium-sized mixed breed eager to love again. New to this but my friends convinced me. Turn-ons: tennis (balls), long walks, and sausages. Turn-offs: cats, flea treatments, and "no." Kibble and canned food got lost... me for Mr. Right (not Mr. Right Now) and's... smart enough to tell me you at top-of-me... Love wins decision, but can't someone who can put put my body. You don't have to be perfumed, but take a man whenever when he says a path

SLAUGHT... AND GYM

FEMALES
Looking for Mr. Goodbone

...just say they don't go down quietly. If you like a girl who knows good food, and loves nothing more than ripping out a silent-but-deadly one in a crowded room on a hot summer day, then I've got a little message for you: *'pffft...'*

I'M SURROUNDED BY FOOLS

Do you hate your friends too? I don't know much, but there's got to be more to life than tugging, rolling around in God-knows-what, and eating rocks (although dirt is decent). If you're tired of innocuous dog-park dates and so much sniffing that goes nowhere, then we might be soul mates. Free most afternoons

MOONDOGGIE, WHERE ARE YOU?

Sun-worshipping beach babe seeks Big Kahuna who loves to soak up the rays and knows when it's time to roll over. Sunsets, bonfires, gnarly waves, and corn dogs float my boat. Man thongs, hairy backs, and muscleheads move on. Let's duck under the beach umbrella and dig our own love castle. No sk8ers please—get a life

CLASSIC BLACK PEARL

Elegant supper club—I'm there with friends—my ears in a casual updo and sporting some silk pajamas—moonlit balcony—I step out for a breath—lost in the distant whir of the orchestra and the scent of jasmine—you startle me from the shadows—we banter—the city below is asleep to our electricity. Dare we dance? A stolen kiss. We search for words but don't seem to need them. Without warning the dawn peeks over the skyline and *it* has begun. That's how I see it ... what's your version?

DATING IS HELL

And I'm your angel of mercy. If you're an adventurous down-to-earth guy, let's hook up and I'll fly you around. Nothing doing with the except a few food allergies, and spots, and a persistent whimpering going. Take a walk on the Domestic side, and come snatch my dish.

RED, WHITE, AND YOURS

Just an all-American gal who digs French kissing. Are you my patriotic pet? Our? Then pucker up, bring your leash, and God Bless America. The bigger the better.

EBONY PRINCESS

Waiting to be for king. My girlfriends say my standards are too high. You should see the mutts they date. Im gettin' strong, intelligent, generous, sexy, clean, funny, mustached. I am snooty. I've had my share of so-so boys. Where's my man? Groomed with claws. P.S. I love massage

CHUB WANTS TO BE CHASED

Middle-aged, plus-sized playmate voracious...

EVER BEEN KISSED BY A SCORPIO?

Medium-sized mixed breed eager to love again. New to this but my friends convinced me. Turn-ons: tennis (balls), long walks, and Snausages. Turn-offs: cats, flea treatments, and "no." Kibble and canned-food girl looking for Mr. Right (NOT Mr. Right Now) who's smart enough to let me win at tug-of-war. Done some modeling, but want someone who can see past my looks. You don't have to be pedigreed, but I like a man who knows when he needs a bath.

FLATULENT AND FUN

Fatty meats, broccoli, certain cheeses. Let's just say they don't go down quietly. If you like a girl who knows good food, and loves nothing more than ripping out a silent-but-deadly one in a crowded room on a hot summer day, then I've got a little message for you: *"pfffft . . ."*

I'M SURROUNDED BY FOOLS

Do you hate your friends too? I don't know much, but there's got to be more to life than tugging, rolling around in God-knows-what, and eating rocks (although dirt is decent). If you're tired of innocuous dog-park dates and so much sniffing that goes nowhere, then we might be soul mates. Free most afternoons.

MOONDOGGIE, WHERE ARE YOU?

Sun-worshipping beach babe seeks Big Kahuna who loves to soak up the rays and knows when it's time to roll over. Sunsets, bonfires, gnarly waves, and corn dogs float my boat. Man thongs, hairy backs, and muscleheads move on. Let's duck under the beach umbrella and dig our own love castle. No sk8ers please—get a life.

CLASSIC BLACK PEARL

Elegant supper club—I'm there with friends—my ears in a casual updo and sporting silk pajamas—moonlit balcony—I step out for a breath—lost in the distant whir of the orchestra and the scent of jasmine—you startle me from the shadows—we banter—the city below is asleep to our electricity. Dare we dance? A stolen kiss. We search for words but don't seem to need them. Without warning the dawn peeks over the skyline and *it* has begun. That's how I see it . . . what's your version?

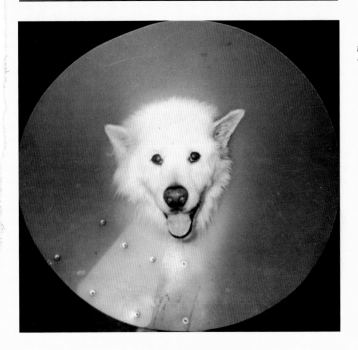

DATING IS HELL

And I'm your angel of mercy. If you're an adventurous down-to-earth sign, let's hook up and I'll fly you around. Nothing wrong with me except a few food allergies, hot spots, and a persistent rash every spring. Take a walk on the celestial side, and come scratch my itch.

RED, WHITE, AND YOURS

Just an all-American girl who digs French kissing. Are you my patriotic pet? *Oui?* Then pucker up, bring your leash, and God Bless America. The hairier the better.

EBONY PRINCESS

Waiting for her king. My girlfriends say my standards are too high. You should see the mutts they date. You are: strong, intelligent, generous, sexy, clean, funny, unattached. I am: ready. I've had my share of squeak toys. Where's my man? Respond with plans. P.S.: I love massage.

CHUB WANTS TO BE CHASED

Middle-aged, plus-sized playmate voracious for boy bands and all smoked meats. Will let the right man catch me. If you like what you see and can handle tons of fun, then give this passionate and appreciative lover what she's hungering for. This yo-yo dieter is love starved!

GIVE ME A "TRY"

Pretty pup squad leader seeks handsome jock or other athletic muscleman for sideline skirmishes. Do you have what it takes to give this good-time girl something to really cheer about? Open to all passes and ready to tackle a monogamous relationship if we're both on the same playing field. Let's hit the showers and see if we can take it into overtime.

ECHO PARK ARTIST SEEKS MUSE

Bohemian sculptress looking to create future with a model of god-dess proportions. If you know the true Zen meaning of the word "sit," then your inspiration is all I'm lacking to truly soar. Work in progress with a passion for all things lovely. Confidence is sexy—not flaunting it is sexier. If you're an organic vegan, there's no limit to the artistry of our girl-on-girl love thang.

FASHION POLICE DOG

Get a "cute" turtleneck for Christmas? Maybe a plaid jacket with snaps and a matching beret? How about those "adorable" quilted antlers everyone thinks are so sweet on a dog? Sound like you? Then go find yourself a Poodle. On the other hand, if you share my eye for progressive style and my nose for the avant-garde, then maybe I'll give you a sniff. I said *maybe*.

COLD PAWS–WARM HEART

X-treme sports femme in touch with my inner wolf. If that's wack to you, then you better bail now. Ever heard the call of the wild and didn't let it go to voice mail? Then I bet we'll connect. Saint Bernards and other fresh-powder buds are hella rad. Let's pee our names in the snow! I'm stoked!

ISLAND LEI

Pineapple heiress on a mainland manhunt. My arranged marriage was annulled and I'm free to find the broad-shouldered military (or ex-military) hero of my dreams. I'm a sucker for a Shepherd in dog tags! If you've got a taste for the tropics, my hula will make you jump through hoops. Use your coconut and say aloha.

VOODOO PRIESTESS

N'Orleans madam with a penchant for other Pugs and a taste for black magic. Aquarian, Stevie Nicks fan who's on the cusp of something truly divine. If you're a Virgo whose moon is rising, then our ultimate destiny may be falling in love. I've tried spells, talismans, and chicken-bone altars to find you. Okay, the chicken was a snack, but you get the picture. Is our harmonic convergence in the cards? Don't let's fight fate.

SINGLE RIDER TO SHARE A CAB AND MORE

Dynamic and fun Upper East Side girl enjoys spa days, dinners out, shopping, and only chews Manolos. Loves Bryant Park on summer nights, cold sesame noodles, and the *Times* in bed on Sundays. Can you get my friends to like you without having to flirt with them? My meter's running, so let's have Snacks in the City.

FIRST CLASS NOW BOARDING

Let's travel the world together and leave our emotional baggage at home. Wash-and-go globetrotter who wants to check my inhibitions and carry on with an international playmate. Member of the mile-high club who will only consider "doodie-free" frequent fliers. Fasten your seat belt, I'm your passport to adventure.

RESCUE MY HEART

Former pound pup wants to share new leash on life with free-spirited height-and-weight proportionate soul mate. Let's duet "Unchained Melody" as we ride with our heads out the car window. Just had my teeth cleaned. Mange is long gone but I've got another itch to scratch. I'm not afraid to get my fur matted, so let's have fun, fun, fun!

IT'S MY TURN

Stardom is in my blood. My grandmother did *Johnny Carson* twice with Joan Embry. My mother booked a guest shot on *21 Jump Street*. They say my father did some stunt work on *Baywatch* but I never knew him (long story). I am: gorgeous, scary talented, ambitious, and unstoppable. You are: connected, not threatened, able to chew with your mouth closed. No musicians, actors, or nonguild writers. Producers and directors move to the head of the line.

I'm the dreamboat that you always wanted you to marry—what are you waiting for? This schlemiel is ready to make a deal.

MR. NICE GUY

Old enough to shave, but still a boy at heart. All my women friends say I'm too great a catch to be single. What gives? Good manners and strong values make for lonely Saturday nights. Nice looking (says my mom), polite, and obedient. Is there a girl out there who wants a traditional guy who still believes in ladies first and the magic of a first sniff? Thank you for your consideration.

DISTEMPERAMENTAL, BUT WORTH IT

No more meds, no more shrinks. I say love me, love my Gemini mood swings. One day I'm sniffing the pretty daisies, and the next I'm gnawing on the remote control, wishing it would rain. Needless to say, I'm an excellent kisser. So look me up, but you probably don't. I hate you. I like classical music. How about you?

2 FAST 2 FURRY

Want to ride shotgun as we cruise down the boulevard of true love? Low-riding, street-smart hombre with four on the floor seeks fast women for high-octane adventures. Let me pop under your hood and make your engine purr. If you know how to check a dip-stick and look good in cha-cha pants, then let's give it a test drive.

COCKEYED OPTIMIST

I still believe in love at first sight, sleeping at the foot of the bed, and "heel." I love how I smell after a bath but can't wait to roll in the mud. A nap in the sun, a scratch behind the ear, and an occasional leg humping are what keep me chasing my tail. I think dog shows should be outlawed, cats are for chasing, and doggie day care is for wimps. Let me know if we see eye to eye.

PURE MUSCLE

All-natural bodybuilder who likes to pump it up with other butt muscle dudes is looking to be worshipped by worked-out males. Very butch—11 pounds of solid muscle—8% body fat—6 pack abs—big guns—trimmed body hair—nice bubble butt. My pec is for real—you should be too. Will be in Tucson for Pride weekend. Show me what you got, boy! Let's party and play?

YOU ARE GETTING SLEEPY . . .

. . . very, very sleepy . . . look deep, deep into my eyes, Miss Sagittarius . . . let go . . . yes . . . do not resist . . . you are mine . . . yes . . . come to me . . . yes . . . bring us a snack . . . that's it . . . that's it . . . sit . . . stay . . . yes . . . good girl.

YOU HAD ME AT ROLL OVER

Be mine, if you are into nightly bedtime, long, lusty Business, and don't think that love is a Mission Impossible, then I'm the Cocktail Wiener dog for you. Do you know what it takes to be my leading lady? Let's jump on the casting couch and find out.

FIVE THINGS I CAN'T LIVE WITHOUT

Broken-in Tennis Balls. Peanut Butter. Public Television. Love. Broken-in Tennis Balls.

GOING MY WAY?

Forward-thinking bon vivant with an eye toward where I've been. Willing to trade my soul for a 9-pack of chicken tenders and a Shiatsu massage. Well traveled; overeducat-ed; lighthearted. Is it true I'm single because I keep looking for a Bond girl in a dive bar? True love and objects in mirror are closer than they appear. I'd rather be at the Hilton in Paris than with Paris Hilton. Life's a trip—pack lightly. Give me a call and start break-ing my heart.

KNOCK KNOCK

Funnyman cutup is seriously looking for you. My comedy may be stand-up, but I'll take my love lyin' down. If fart jokes make you howl and you see the upside of short men, then what are we waiting for? When I tell you you have a beautiful body, will you hold it against me? Let's redefine the whoopee cushion.

SCOOBY DO ME

Gen X, urban hipster dogs Frisbee in the park, classic cartoons, and all things random. Spiritual, not religious—Spunza. Deepak. Kabbalah. I'm a philosophy buff who picks up freelance Seeing Eye shifts for extra cash. If you're looking for nirvana and aren't afraid to chase it for a couple of blocks, let's fetch a couple of chai lattes and see if we connect. The muzzle's just some bling bling, so let's do it!

DIGNITY?

They dress me in a tutu and make me twirl for liver treats. I've been the Easter bunny, a scarecrow, a reindeer (or—ahwer), a lep-rechaun, and a diapered cupid. I had no choice. They were feeding me. Why should you date me? It got you, why?

"DOG" SPELLED BACKWARDS

ME: Sexy. Irresistible. Brilliant. Scorpio. Insatiable. Hot. SEXY. God.
YOU: Lucky.

MIXED NUT

My analyst says I'm cured. Irrational fear of goose down has kept me single for too long—a complicated saga that I look forward to shar-ing. Obsessive-compulsive with all my bis-cuits in a row. Bald patches are filling in nicely and my involuntary paw-washing is in check. Let's get crazy in love.

FIRST CLASS NOW BOARDING

Let's travel the world together and leave our emotional baggage at home. Wash-and-go globetrotter who wants to check my inhibi-tions and carry on with an international play-mate. Member of the mile-high club who will only consider "doodie-free" frequent fliers. Fasten your seat belt. I'm your passport to adventure.

RESCUE MY HEART

Former pound pup wants to share new leash on life with free-spirited height-and-weight proportionate soul mate. Let's duet "Unchained Melody" as we ride with our heads out the car window. Just had my teeth cleaned. Mange is long gone but I've got another itch to scratch. I'm not afraid to get my fur matted, so let's have fun, fun, fun!

IT'S MY TURN

Stardom is in my blood. My grandmother did Johnnie Carson twice and Joan Embry. My mother booked a guest shot on 21 Jump Street. They say my father did some stunt work on Baywatch but I never knew him (long story). I am: gorgeous, scary talented, ambi-tious, and unstoppable. You are: connected, not threatened, able to chew with your mouth closed. No nasty directors, or nonglobal writers. Producers or agents move to the head of the line.

PRINCE, MY DOG

Yo! Yo! Yo! What up, señoritas?! The family is gone and the crib is mine! So let's howl at the moon and roll around on the new carpet. Bring your housebroken, fixed friends, and let's get this thing started! All the food you can eat to the one who can get the refrigera-tor open. Peace out, y'all! Aargh!!

MURRAY THE K-9

Orthodox mensch who's tired of shvitzing over finding the perfect Jewish-American Poodle. Willing to reform my love life to the right. Easily-anoated shiksa with broad, child-bearing hips, I'll walk you from the shore,

PARTY AT MY HOUSE!

Yo! Yo! Yo! What up, senoritas?! The family is gone and the crib is mine! So let's howl at the moon and roll around on the new carpet. Bring your housebroken, fixed friends, and let's get this thing started! All the food you can eat to the one who can get the refrigerator open. Peace out, y'all! Aaigght?

MURRAY THE K-9

Orthodox mensch who's tired of shvitzing over finding the perfect Jewish-American Poodle. Willing to reform my love life for the right family-oriented shiksa with broad, child-bearing hips. I'll walk away from the chuppah and the hoopla if you are my chosen one. I'm the dreamboat that your mother wants you to marry—what are you waiting for? This schlemiel is ready to make a deal.

MR. NICE GUY

Old enough to shave, but still a boy at heart. All my women friends say I'm too great a catch to be single. What gives? Good manners and strong values make for lonely Saturday nights. Nice looking (says my mom), polite, and obedient. Is there a girl out there who wants a traditional guy who still believes in ladies first and the magic of a first sniff? Thank you for your consideration.

DISTEMPERAMENTAL, BUT WORTH IT

No more meds, no more shrinks. I say love me, love my Gemini mood swings. One day I'm sniffing the pretty daisies, and the next I'm gnawing on the remote control, wishing it would rain. Needless to say, I'm an excellent kisser. So look me up, but you probably won't. I hate you. I like classical music. How about you?

2 FAST 2 FURRY

Want to ride shotgun as we cruise down the boulevard of true love? Low-riding, street-smart hombre with four on the floor seeks fast women for high-octane adventures. Let me pop under your hood and make your engine purr. If you know how to check a dipstick and look good in cha-cha pants, then let's give it a test drive.

COCKEYED OPTIMIST

I still believe in love at first sight, sleeping at the foot of the bed, and "heel." I love how I smell after a bath but can't wait to roll in the mud. A nap in the sun, a scratch behind the ear, and an occasional leg hump are what keep me chasing my tail. I think dog shows should be outlawed, cats are for chasing, and doggie day care is for wimps. Let me know if we see eye to eye.

PURE MUSCLE

All-natural bodybuilder who likes to pump it up with other buff
muscle dudes is looking to be worshipped by worked-out hunks.
Very butch—11 pounds of solid muscle—8% body fat—6-pack
abs—big guns—trimmed body hair—nice bubble butt. My pic is
for real—you should be too. Will be in Tucson for Pride weekend.
Show me what you got, boy! Let's party and play!

YOU ARE GETTING SLEEPY . . .

. . . very, very sleepy . . . look deep, deep into my eyes, Miss
Sagittarius . . . let go . . . yes . . . do not resist . . . you are mine . . .
yes . . . come to me . . . yes . . . bring us a snack . . . that's it . . .
that's it . . . sit . . . stay . . . yes . . . good girl . . .

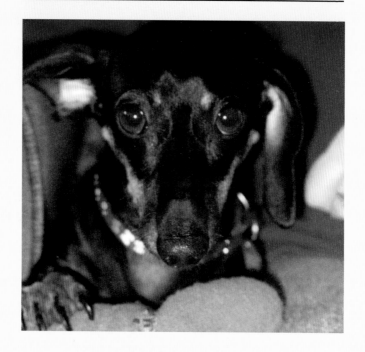

YOU HAD ME AT ROLL OVER

Top Dog, Tom Cruise look-alike, seeks sassy Penelope Cruz-ish Chihuahua to pull three G's with. If you dig Jerky McGuire, doing Risky Business, and don't think that love is a Mission Impossible, then I'm the Cocktail Wiener dog for you. Do you have what it takes to be my leading lady? Let's jump on the casting couch and find out.

FIVE THINGS I CAN'T LIVE WITHOUT
Broken-in Tennis Balls. Peanut Butter. Public Television. Love.
Broken-in Tennis Balls.

OBJECTS IN MIRROR ARE
CLOSER THAN THEY APPEAR

GOING MY WAY?

Forward-thinking bon vivant with an eye toward where I've been. Willing to trade my soul for a 9-pack of chicken tenders and a Shiatsu massage. Well traveled, overeducated, lighthearted. Is it true I'm single because I keep looking for a Bond girl in a dive bar? True love and objects in mirror are closer than they appear. I'd rather be at the Hilton in Paris than with Paris Hilton. Life's a trip—pack lightly. Give me a call and start breaking my heart.

KNOCK KNOCK

Funnyman cutup is seriously looking for you. My comedy may be stand-up, but I'll take my love lyin' down. If fart jokes make you howl and you see the upside of short men, then what are we waiting for? When I tell you you have a beautiful body, will you hold it against me?! Let's redefine the whoopee cushion.

SCOOBY DO ME

Gen X, urban hipster digs Frisbee in the park, classic cartoons, and all things random. Spiritual, not religious—Spinoza, Deepak. Kabbalah. I'm a philosophy buff who picks up freelance Seeing Eye shifts for extra cash. If you're looking for nirvana and aren't afraid to chase it for a couple of blocks, let's fetch a couple of chai lattes and see if we connect. The muzzle's just some bling bling, so let's do it!!

DIGNITY?

They dress me in a tutu and make me twirl for liver treats. I've been the Easter bunny, a scarecrow, a reindeer (see above), a leprechaun, and a diapered cupid. I had no choice. They were feeding me. Why should you date me? If not you, who?

"DOG" SPELLED BACKWARDS

ME: Sexy. Irresistible. Brilliant. Scorpio. Insatiable. Hot. SEXY. God.
YOU: Lucky.

MIXED NUT

My analyst says I'm cured. Irrational fear of goose down has kept me single too long—a complicated saga that I look forward to sharing. Obsessive-compulsive with all my biscuits in a row. Bald patches are filling in nicely and my involuntary paw-washing is in check. Let's get crazy in love.

I'M A CLICHÉ

I stick my head out the car window. I sniff tree trunks, eat grass, and have an eclectic collection of rawhide bonery. I sleep with my head between the couch cushions, and get a cup of vanilla ice cream every year for my birthday. No apologies, no regrets. I'm a dog doing my job, looking for a pooch who appreciates my handiwork.

CELIBATE AND FETCHING

I was a sex addict; now I fetch. Big sticks, small sticks, birch, pine, oak, table legs. 24/7. I do get lonely for a lady. (Just because I'm on a diet doesn't mean I can't look at the menu . . .) If a nice guy working through his sexual issues sounds like your cup of tea, then let's bring home some lumber together.

LAST CALL

My trust fund has run out. The party has moved on. Reformed Lothario, toilet-breathed Jack Russell finally ready to settle down by a warm fire for long evenings of pigs' ears and Pictionary. Are you the lady who can help me forget the bodacious pups of my mad-dog past? If you're old and ugly, please be rich.

old enough to shave, but still a boy at heart. All my women friends say I'm too great a catch to be single. What gives? Good manners and strong values make for lonely Saturday nights. Nice looking (says my mom), polite, and obedient. Is there a girl out there who wants a traditional guy who still believes in ladies first and the magic of a first sniff? Thank you for your consideration.

DISTEMPERAMENTAL, BUT WORTH IT
No more meds, no more shows. I say love me, love my Gemini mood swings. One day I'm sniffing the pretty daisies, and the next I'm gnawing on the remote control, wishing it would rain. Needless to say, I'm an excellent kisser. So look me up, but you probably won't. I hate you. I like classical music. How about you?

2 FAST 2 FURRY
Want to ride shotgun as we cruise down the boulevard of true love? Low-riding, street-smart bonbire with four on the floor seeks fast women for high-octane adventures. Let me pop under your hood and make your engine purr. If you know how to check a dipstick and look good in cha-cha pants, then let's give it a test drive.

COCKEYED OPTIMIST
I still believe in love at first sight, sleeping at the foot of the bed, and "heel." I love how I smell after a bath but can't wait to roll in the mud. A nap in the sun, a scratch behind the ear, and an occasional leg hump are what keep me chasing my tail. I think dog shows should be outlawed, cats are for chasing and doggie day care is for vamps. Let me know if we see eye to eye.

PURE MUSCLE
All-natural bodybuilder who likes to pump it up with other buff muscle dudes is looking to be worshipped by worked-out hunks. Very butch — 11 pounds of solid muscle — 8% body fat — 6-pack abs — big guns — trimmed booty hair — nice bubble butt. My pic is for real — you should be too. Will be in Tucson for Pride weekend. Show me what you got, boy! Let's party and play!

YOU ARE GETTING SLEEPY . . .
. . . very, very sleepy . . . look deep, deep into my eyes, kiss Sagittarius . . . I t go . . . yes . . . do not resist . . . you are done . . . yes . . . come to me . . . yes . . . bring us a snack that's it . . . that's it . . . sit . . . stay . . . yes . . . good girl . . .

YOU HAD ME AT ROLL OVER
Top Dog, Tom Cruise look-alike, seeks skinny Penelope Cruz-ish Chihuahua to pull three G's with. If you dig Jerky McGuire, doing Risky Business, and don't think that love is a

to be my bitch, go, casting couch and find out.

FIVE THINGS I CAN'T LIVE WITHOUT
Broken-in Tennis Balls. Peanut Butter. Public Television. Love. Broken-in Tennis Balls.

GOING MY WAY?
Forward-thinking bon vivant with an eye toward where I've been. Willing to trade my soul for a 9-pack of chicken tenders and a Shiatsu massage. Well traveled, overeducated, lighthearted. Is it true I'm single because I keep looking for a Bond girl in a dive bar? True love and objects in mirror are closer than they appear. I'd rather be at the Hilton in Paris than with Paris Hilton. Life's a trip — pack lightly. Give me a call and start breaking my heart.

KNOCK KNOCK
Funnyman cutup is seriously looking for you. My comedy may be stand-up, but I'll take my love lyin' down. It fart jokes make you howl and you see the upside of short men, then what are we waiting for? When I tell you you have a beautiful body, will you hold it against me?! Let's redefine the whoopee cushion.

SCOOBY DO ME
Gen X, urban hipster digs Frisbee in the park, classic cartoons, and all things random. Spiritual, not religious—Spinoza, Deepak, Kabbalah. I'm a philosophy buff who picks up freelance Seeing Eye shifts for extra cash. If you're looking for nirvana and aren't afraid to chase it for a couple of blocks, let's fetch a couple of chai lattes and see if we connect. The muzzle's just some bling bling, so let's do it!

DIGNITY?
They dress me in a tutu and make me twirl for liver treats. I've been the Easter bunny, a scarecrow, a reindeer (see above), a leprechaun, and a diapered cupid. I had no choice. They were feeding me. Why should you date me? It will, you, who?

"DOG" SPELLED BACKWARDS
ME, Sexy, Irresistible, Brilliant, Scorpio, Insatiable, Hot, SEXY, God.
YOU, Lucky.

MIXED NUT
My analyst says I'm cured, but my fear of goose down has kept me single too long — a complicated saga that I look forward to sharing. Obsessive-compulsive with all my biscuits in a row. Bald patches are hiding in nicely and my involuntary paw-washing is in check. Let's go crazy in love.

I'M A CLICHE
I stick my head out the car window. I sniff tree trunks, eat grass, and have an eclectic

birthday. No apologies, no regrets. I'm a dog doing my job, looking for a pooch who appreciates my handiwork.

CELIBATE AND FETCHING
I was a sex addict; now I fetch. Big sticks, small sticks, birch, pine, oak, table legs 24/7. I do get lonely for a lady. (Just because I'm on a diet doesn't mean I can't look at the menu . . .) If a nice guy working through his sexual issues sounds like your cup of tea, then let's bring home some lumber together.

LAST CALL
My trust fund has run out. The party has moved on. Reformed Lothario, toilet-breathed Jack Russell finally ready to settle down by a warm fire for long evenings of pigs ears and Pictionary. Are you the lady who can help me forget the bodacious pups of my mad-dog past? If you reply and apply, please be rich.

PUPPY LOVE

Still Going on the Paper

NEW LEASH . . .
Think backyards are for sissies? Do you get off on humans picking up after you with those little plastic bags? (It's the law!) If you're a bitch who loves the smell of day-old weenie water, midtown hydrants, and a nice summer garbage strike, then let's hook up and do Gotham doggy style. You got a problem with that??

DON'T TELL MY DADDY
Barely legal freshman who's looking for an education to love. Boys at home were all thumbs. I need a sophisticated city fella to show me the finer points of romance. Are you generous enough to share your experience with this petite and insatiable coed? Little thing like me could get lost in this expensive town without a big, strong escort. Professional gents only, please — married men encouraged.

HE'S NEVER WRONG
My imaginary friend had a dream about you last night. You had a silky coat and a sexy bark. You ate grass and liver and hated gunfights on TV and having your teeth cleaned. You loved cheese, pepperoni sticks, and especially me. Are you too good to be

NEW YORK NOOKIE

Think backyards are for sissies? Do you get off on humans picking up after you with those little plastic bags? (It's the law!) If you're a bitch who loves the smell of day-old weenie water, midtown hydrants, and a nice summer garbage strike, then let's hook up and do Gotham doggy style. You got a problem with that??

DON'T TELL MY DADDY

Barely legal freshman who's looking for an education in love. Boys at home were all thumbs—I need a sophisticated city fella to show me the finer points of romance. Are you generous enough to share your experience with this petite and insatiable coed? Little thing like me could get lost in this expensive town without a big, strong escort. Professional gents only, please—married men encouraged.

HE'S NEVER WRONG

My imaginary friend had a dream about you last night. You had a silky coat and a sexy bark. You ate grass and liver and hated gunfights on TV and having your teeth cleaned. You loved cheese, pepperoni sticks, and especially me. Are you too good to be true? Fine with me. That's what imaginary friends are for—to find you imaginary girlfriends.

I CHEW
You?

REBEL WITH 4 PAWS

Crate-trained Catholic schoolgirl who is a confirmed hell-raiser—
muzzle that, Sister Dorothea! What you see is what you get from
this straight-shooting Spaniel mix who's not afraid to jump on
people or picnic tables. Know right from wrong but willing to trade
risk for reward. Are you a sweet-talking, roughneck thrill seeker who
likes to throw down? Gimme a shout and come stare danger down
the snout.

HAVE WE MET?

I was your randy Roman senator, your lovelorn manservant in war-torn China, your lusty courtesan in sixteenth-century Venice. Ring any bells? Are we soul mates, tumbling through lifetimes together? Then come find me like always, my love, and let's see what passions we can stir this go-round. If you're not a dog now too, let's skip it till next time.

HOT MAMAS SERVED FRESH DAILY

Young buck eager for a mature woman to show him the ropes. I'm all ears when it comes to what you have to teach me. If you're not getting the attention you deserve at home, come on over and we'll put those hot flashes to good use. Let's take a walk on the wild side. I'm discreet, with my own place for one-time-only or regular rendezvous.

LOSIN' MY "BOYS"

The appointment has been made. The fix is in. What I need now is one night of unneutered passion while I still have my manhood. Are you spayed? Then you know where I'm coming from. I don't care about your breed, your life story, or your favorite cheese. I just want to love you and not think about tomorrow.

IT'S MY TURN

Stardom is in my blood. My grandmother did *Johnny Carson* twice with Joan Embry. My mother booked a guest shot on *21 Jump Street*. They say my father did some stunt work on *Baywatch* but I never knew him (long story). I am: gorgeous, scary talented, ambitious, and unstoppable. You are: connected, not threatened, able to chew with your mouth closed. No musicians, actors, or nonguild writers. Producers and directors move to the head of the line.

MALES
Alpha Dogs

PARTY AT MY HOUSE!

Yo! Yo! Yo! What up, senoritas?! The family is gone and the crib is mine! So let's howl at the moon and roll around on the new carpet. Bring your housebroken, fixed friends, and let's get this thing started! All the food you can eat to the one who can get the refrigerator open. Peace out, y'all!

MURRAY THE K-9

Orthodox mensch who's tired of shvitzing over finding the perfect Jewish-American Poodle. Willing to reform my love life for the right family-oriented shiksa with broad, child-bearing hips. I'll walk away from the chuppah and the hoopla if you are my chosen one. I'm the dreamboat that your mother wants you to marry—what are you waiting for? This schlemiel is ready to make a deal.

MR. NICE GUY

Old enough to shave, but still a boy at heart. All my women friends say I'm too great a catch to be single. What gives? Good manners and strong values make for lonely Saturday nights. Nice looking (says my mom), polite, and obedient. Is there a girl out there who wants a traditional guy who still believes in ladies first and the magic of a first kiss? Thank you for your consideration.

DISTEMPERAMENTAL, BUT WORTH IT

No more meds, no more shrinks, I say love me, love my Gemini mood swings. One day I'm sniffing the pretty daisies, and the next I'm gnawing on the remote control, wishing it would rain. Needless to say, I'm an excellent kisser. So look me up, but you probably won't. I hate you. I like classical music. How about you?

2 FAST 2 FURRY

Want to ride shotgun as we cruise down the boulevard of true love? Low-riding, street-smart hombre with *fuor* on the floor seeks

---

me pop under your hood and make your engine purr. If you know how to check a dip-stick and look good in cha-cha pants, then let's give it a test drive.

COCKEYED OPTIMIST

I still believe in love at first sight, sleeping at the foot of the bed, and "heel." I love how I smell after a bath but can't wait to roll in the mud. A nap in the sun, a scratch behind the ear, and an occasional leg hump are what keep me chasing my tail. I think dog shows should be outlawed, cats are for chasing, and doggie day care is for wimps. Let me know if we see eye to eye.

PURE MUSCLE

All-natural bodybuilder who likes to pump it up with other buff muscle dudes is looking to be worshipped by worked-out hunks. Very butch—11 pounds of solid muscle—8% body fat—6-pack abs—big guns—trimmed body hair—nice bubble butt. My pic is for real—you should be too. Will be in Tucson for Pride weekend. Show me what you got, boy! Let's party and play!

YOU ARE GETTING SLEEPY . . .

. . . very, very sleepy . . . look deep, deep into my eyes. Miss Sagittarius . . . let go . . . yes . . . do not resist . . . you are mine . . . yes . . . come to me . . . yes . . . bring us a snack . . . that's it . . . that's it . . . sit . . . stay . . . yes . . . good girl . .

YOU HAD ME AT ROLL OVER

Top Dog. Tom Cruise look-alike. seeks sassy Penelope Cruz-ish Chihuahua to pull three G's with. If you dig Jerky McGuire, doing *Risky Business*, and don't think that love is a *Mission Impossible*, then I'm the Cocktail Wiener dog for you. Do you have what it takes to be my leading lady? Let's jump on the casting couch and find out.

FIVE THINGS I CAN'T LIVE WITHOUT

Broken-in Tennis Balls. Peanut Butter. Public Television. Love. Broken-in Tennis Balls.

GOING MY WAY?

Forward-thinking bon vivant with an eye toward where I've been. Willing to trade my soul for a 9-pack of chicken tenders and a Shiatsu massage. Well traveled, overeducated, lighthearted. Is it true I'm single because I keep looking for a Bond girl in a dive bar? True love and objects in mirror are closer than they appear. I'd rather be at the Hilton in Paris than with Paris Hilton. Life's a trip—pack lightly. Give me a call and start breaking my heart.

KNOCK KNOCK

Funnyman cutup is seriously looking for you. My comedy may be stand-up, but I'll take my love lyin' down. If fart jokes make you howl

---

have a beautiful body, will you hold it against me? Let's redefine the whoopee cushion.

SCOOBY DO ME

Gen X, urban hipster digs Frisbee in the park, classic cartoons, and things random. Spiritual, not religious—Spinoza, Deepak, Kabbalah. I'm a philosophy buff who picks up freelance Seeing Eye shifts for extra cash. If you're looking for nirvana and aren't afraid to chase it for a couple of blocks, let's fetch a couple of chai lattes and see if we connect. The muzzle's just some bling bling, so let's do it?!

DIGNITY?

They dress me in a tutu and make me twirl for liver treats. I've been the Easter bunny, a scarecrow, a reindeer (see above), a leprechaun, and a diapered cupid. I had no choice. They were feeding me. Why should you date me? If not you, who?

"DOG" SPELLED BACKWARDS

ME: Sexy. Irresistible. Brilliant. Scorpio. Insatiable. Hot. SEXY. God.
YOU: Lucky.

MIXED NUT

My analyst says I'm cured. Irrational fear of goose down has kept me single too long—a complicated saga that I look forward to sharing. Obsessive-compulsive with all my biscuits in a row. Bald patches are filling in nicely and my involuntary paw-washing is in check. Let's get crazy in love.

I'M A CLICHÉ

I stick my head out the car window. I sniff tree trunks, eat grass, and have an eclectic collection of rawhide bones. I sleep with my head between the couch cushions, and get a cup of vanilla ice cream every year for my birthday. No apologies, no regrets. I'm a dog doing my job, looking for a pooch who appreciates my handiwork.

CELIBATE AND FETCHING

I was a sex addict: now I fetch. Big sticks, small sticks, birch, pine, oak, table legs. 24/7. I do get lonely for a lady. (Just because I'm on a diet doesn't mean I can't look at the menu . . .) If a nice guy working through his sexual issues sounds like your cup of tea, then let's bring home some lumber together.

LAST CALL

My trust fund has run out. The party has moved on. Reformed Lothario, toilet-breathed Jack Russell finally ready to settle down by a warm fire for long evenings of pigs ears and Pictionary. Are you the lady who can help me forget the bodacious pups of my mad-dog past? If you're old and ugly, please be rich.

PUPPY LOVE

...ninb backyards are for sissies. Do you get off on humans picking up after you with those little plastic bags? (It's the law!) If you're a bitch who loves the smell of day-old weenie water, midtown hydrants, and a ripe summer garbage strike, then let's hook up and do Gotham doggy style. You got a problem with that?

DON'T TELL MY DADDY
Barely legal freshman who's looking for an education in love. Boys at home were all thumbs -- I need a sophisticated city fella to show me the finer points of romance. Are you generous enough to share your experiences with this petite and insatiable coed? Lose anything like me could get lost in this expansive town without a big strong escort. Professional gents only, please—married men encouraged.

HE'S NEVER WRONG
My imaginary friend had a dream about me last night. You had a silky coat, and a sexy bark. You ate grass, and liver, and hated gunfights on TV, and having your teeth cleaned. You loved cheese, pepperoni sticks, and especially me. Are you too good to be true? Fine with me. That's what imaginary friends are for—to find you imaginary girlfriends.

I CHEW
You?

REBEL WITH 4 PAWS
Crate-trained Catholic schoolgirl who is a confirmed hell-raiser—muzzle that, Sister Dorothea! What you see is what you get from this straight-shooting Spaniel mix who's not afraid to jump on police tables. Know right from wrong but willing to trade risk for reward. Are you a sweet-talking, rough-neck thrill seeker who likes to throw down? Gimme a shout and come stare danger down the snout.

HAVE WE MET?
I was your randy Roman Senator, your loveliest manservant in war-torn China, your lusty courtesan in sixteenth-century Venice. Ring any bells? Are we soul mates, tumbling through lifetimes together? Then come find me like always, my love, and let's see what passions we can stir this go-round. If you're not a dog now too, let's skip it till next time.

HOT MAMMAS SERVED FRESH DAILY
Young buck eager for a mature woman to show him the ropes. I'm a stud when it comes to what you have to teach me. If you're not getting the attention you deserve at home, come on over and we'll put those hot flashes to good use. Let's take a walk on the wild side. I'm discreet, with my own place for...

The appointment has been made, the nic is in. What I need now is one night of unneutered passion while I still have my manhood. Are you spayed? Then you know where I'm coming from. I don't care about your breed, your life story, or your favorite cheese. I just want to love you and not think about tomorrow.

BEEN AROUND THE BLOCK
The AARF Generation

A FEW MOVES LEFT
Like rap to Mozart, you're the glucosamine tablet in a cheese cube? Me too. I want a sniff and tumble with a babe who remembers life before the Macarena and campaign-finance reform. Looks not important, but if you're a long-legged Ann-Margret type, let's smooch while I still have my teeth. No Corgis.

COUNTRY FELLER
Down-home farm boy fixin' to come a-courtin'. If you've ever slept under the stars with a body full of s'mores, then you know what stokes my fire. Sturdy, kind heart, good morals, and one helluva fox chaser. Lookin' to lasso a pretty little thang that knows how to rustle up a possum, likes a bath on Sunday, and doesn't mind being seen in town with a square like me.

CLEAN-LIVING DIRTY BLONDE
No nonsense, empty-nested mother of six with great teeth and teeth seeks meaningless relationship with a very naughty boy. No hackers, biters, or stupid pet tricks—been there, done that. The eye? I'll tell you all about it over dinner . . . wink, wink.

SINGLE DAD
I have one young son who is my pride and joy. He fills my life, but there's always room for more. Legally I'm an adult—but really a kid at heart. I'm not a Don Johnson but not so bad too. I get lonely sometimes and wish that I could have someone to share my thoughts with. Your interests are mine if I'm interested in you. Prefer single mom so the priorities are...

THE SCENT OF TRUE LOVE
Down-to-earth Bloodhound with a nose for bull. Had a near-death experience when I choked on a biscuit. Now I'd rather watch the squirrels than chase them. On the trail of a new romantic partner who is loving, licensed, and knows how to make a huntin' dog's jowls drop. If you like the simple life, there's room for two on my front porch. Bichon Frises? I reckon not.

WHO'S YOUR DADDY?
I've had enough of old broads trying to teach me new tricks. Now I want 'em young and stupid. If you haven't even broken in your first squeaky toy and don't understand "no" yet, then maybe we can play. Just be paper-trained.

BULLET UNDER CONSTRUCTION
Recently out lesbian mom looking to get my feet wet in the waters of Sappho sisterhood. I enjoy lumberyards, HGTV, sunsets, and anything from Eva Cassidy. You be lipstick, gentle, and understanding of an old dog on a new path. Looking forward to sharing the rainbow of my orgasm with someone other than myself. Katie Couric look-alikes a real +.

BLUE-COLLAR CASTLE
Doublewide King ready to crown my new Queen. Honest-living, honest-loving low-truck assist wants someone to share the good times with. Got 2 kids that live with their mother in Prescott. Not looking for more. Full-figure girls make me smile. Writing ain't my thing, so if you like what you see and have all your teeth, then hit me up and we'll take it from there.

IT'S NEVER TOO LATE
Long-in-the-tooth Tramp type looking for a Lady to love. Seen the U.S. of A. from the cab of an 18-wheeler. Had the good fortune to pee in 43 different states, with pictures to prove it. Now lookin' to put down some roots and pooper-scoop my own backyard. Ready for the picket fence, home-cooked meals, and a little to teach how to play ball. Stable provider—full benefits and enough savings to stake our future. Will you be part of it?

SUPER SENIOR
Former stray seeks soul mate to spend twilight with. Friends first and then . . . ? Cataracts have given me the chance to look inside, and I like what I see. Are you what else I'm looking for? Abusers and neglecters move on. This old-timer's seen it all. Surprise me.

HAVE YOU SEEN MY HEART?
Recently ended a long-term relationship or, rather, it ended me. I'm giving love one last try before I bury my heart for good. I don't...

A FEW MOVES LEFT

Like rap music? Me neither. Take your glucosamine tablet in a
cheese cube? Me too. I want a sniff and tumble with a babe who
remembers life before the Macarena and campaign-finance reform.
Looks not important, but if you're a long-legged Ann-Margret type,
let's smooch while I still have my teeth. No Corgis.

COUNTRY FELLER

Down-home farm boy fixin' to come a-courtin'. If you've ever slept under the stars with a belly full of s'mores, then you know what stokes my fire. Sturdy, kind heart, good morals, and one helluva fox chaser. Lookin' to lasso a pretty little thing that knows how to rustle up a possum, likes a bath on Sunday, and doesn't mind being seen in town with a square like me.

CLEAN-LIVING DIRTY BLONDE

No-nonsense, empty-nested mother of six with great teets and teeth seeks meaningless relationship with a very naughty boy. No barkers, biters, or stupid pet tricks—been there, done that. The eye? I'll tell you all about it over dinner . . . wink, wink.

SINGLE DAD

I have one young son who is my pride and joy. He fills my life, but there's always room for more. Legally I'm an adult—but really a kid at heart. I'm not a Don Johnson but not so bad too. I get lonely sometimes and wish that I could have someone to share my thoughts with. Your interests are mine if I'm interested in you. Prefer single mom so the priorities are commonly understood. I would like to hear from you.

THE SCENT OF TRUE LOVE

Down-to-earth Bloodhound with a nose for bull. Had a near-death experience when I choked on a biscuit. Now I'd rather watch the squirrels than chase them. On the trail of a new romantic partner who is loving, licensed, and knows how to make a huntin' dog's jowls drop. If you like the simple life, there's room for two on my front porch. Bichon Frises? I reckon not.

WHO'S YOUR DADDY?

I've had enough of old broads trying to teach me new tricks. Now I want 'em young and stupid. If you haven't even broken in your first squeaky toy and don't understand "no" yet, then maybe we can play. Just be paper trained.

MULLET UNDER CONSTRUCTION

Recently out lesbian mom looking to get my feet wet in the waters of Sappho sisterhood. I enjoy lumberyards, HGTV, sunsets, and anything from Eva Cassidy. You be lipstick, gentle, and understanding of an old dog on a new path. Looking forward to sharing the rainbow of my orgasm with someone other than myself. Katie Couric look-alikes a real +.

BLUE-COLLAR CASTLE

Doublewide King ready to crown my new Queen. Honest-living, honest-loving tow-truck assist wants someone to share the good times with. Got 2 kids that live with their mother in Prescott. Not looking for more. Full-figure girls make me smile. Writing ain't my thing, so if you like what you see and have all your teeth, then hit me up and we'll take it from there.

IT'S NEVER TOO LATE

Long-in-the-tooth Tramp type looking for a Lady to love. Seen the U.S. of A. from the cab of an 18-wheeler. Had the good fortune to pee in 43 different states, with pictures to prove it. Now lookin' to put down some roots and pooper-scoop my own backyard. Ready for the picket fence, home-cooked meals, and a litter to teach how to play ball. Stable provider—full benefits and enough savings to stake our future. Will you be part of it?

SUPER SENIOR

Former stray seeks soul mate to spend twilight with. Friends first
and then . . . ? Cataracts have given me the chance to look inside,
and I like what I see. Are you what else I'm looking for? Abusers
and neglecters move on. This old-timer's seen it all. Surprise me.

HAVE YOU SEEN MY HEART?

Recently ended a long-term relationship or, rather, it ended me.
I'm giving love one last try before I bury my heart for good. I don't
help the blind cross the street or save children from burning
buildings. I'm just a dog asking another dog to love me. Interested?
Then start digging.

I'VE GOT ONE LEFT AFTER MY DIVORCE

Recently single and back in circulation. Not bitter—just wiser.
A woman with too much time on her hands is bound to stray—
especially when your freeloading half brother lives with you. I've
cleaned house (God forbid she ever did) and am ready to move on.
Cheating, lying, selfish, controlling, vindictive ballbusters need
not apply.

scarecrow, a reindeer (see above), a leprechaun, and a diapered cupid. I had no
choice. They were feeding me. Why should you
date me? If not you, who?

"DOG" SPELLED BACKWARDS

ME: Sexy. Irresistible. Brilliant. Scorpio.
Insatiable. Hot. SEXY. God.
YOU: Lucky.

MIXED NUT

My analyst says I'm cured. Irrational fear of
goose down has kept me single too long—a
complicated saga that I look forward to sharing. Obsessive-compulsive with all my biscuits in a row. Bald patches are filling in
nicely and my involuntary paw-washing is in
check. Let's get crazy in love.

I'M A CLICHE

I stick my head out the car window. I sniff
tree trunks, eat grass, and have an eclectic
collection of rawhide bones. I sleep with my
head between the couch cushions, and get a
cup of vanilla ice cream every year for my
birthday. No apologies, no regrets. I'm a dog
doing my job, looking for a pooch who appreciates my handiwork.

CELIBATE AND FETCHING

I was a sex addict, now I fetch. Big sticks,
small sticks, birch, pine, oak, table legs.
24/7. I do get lonely for a lady. (Just because
I'm on a diet doesn't mean I can't look at the
menu . . .) If a nice guy working through his
sexual issues sounds like your cup of tea,
then let's bring home some lumber together.

LAST CALL

My trust fund has run out. The party has
moved on. Reformed Lothario, toilet-breathed
Jack Russell finally ready to settle down by a
warm fire for long evenings of pigs ears and
Pictionary. Are you the lady who can help me
forget the bodacious pups of my mad-dog
past? If you're old and ugly, please be rich.

PUPPY LOVE
Still Going on the Paper

NEW YORK NOOKIE

Think backyards are for sissies? Do you get
off on humans picking up after you with
those little plastic bags? (It's the law!) If
you're a bitch who loves the smell of day-old
weenie water, midtown hydrants, and a nice
summer garbage stink, then let's hook up
and do Gotham doggy style. You got a problem with that??

DON'T TELL MY DADDY

Barely legal freshman who's looking for an
education in love. Boys at home were all
thumbs—I need a sophisticated city fella to
show me the finer points of romance. Are you

---

thing like me could get lost in this expensive
town without a big strong escort. Professional
gents only, please—married men encouraged.

HE'S NEVER WRONG

My imaginary friend had a dream about you
last night. You had a silky coat, and a sexy
bark. You ate grass, and liver, and hated
gunfights on TV, and having your teeth
cleaned. You loved cheese, pepperoni sticks,
and especially me. Are you too good to be
true? Fine with me. That's what imaginary
friends are for—to find you imaginary girlfriends.

I CHEW

You?

REBEL WITH 4 PAWS

Crate-trained Catholic schoolgirl who is a
confirmed belly-licker—muzzle that, Sister
Dorothea! What you see is what you get from
this straight-shooting Spaniel mix who's not
afraid to jump on people or picnic tables.
Know right from wrong but willing to trade
risk for reward. Are you a sweet-talking,
rough-neck thrill seeker who likes to throw
down? Gimme a shout and come stare danger down the snout.

HAVE WE MET?

I was your randy Roman senator, your lovelorn
manservant in war-torn China, your lusty
courtesan in sixteenth-century Venice. Ring
any bells? Are we soul mates, tumbling
through lifetimes together? Then come find
me like always, my love, and let's see what
passions we can stir this go-round. If you're
not a dog now too, let's skip it till next time.

HOT MAMMAS SERVED FRESH DAILY

Young buck eager for a mature woman to
show him the ropes. I'm all ears when it
comes to what you have to teach me. If you're
not getting the attention you deserve at
home, come on over and we'll put those hot
flashes to good use. Let's take a walk on the
wild side. I'm discreet, with my own place for
one-time-only or regular rendezvous.

LOSIN' MY "BOYS"

The appointment has been made. The fix is
in. What I need now is one night of
unneutered passion while I still have my
manhood. Are you spayed? Then you know
where I'm coming from. I don't care about
your breed, your life story, or your favorite
cheese. I just want to love you and not think
about tomorrow.

BEEN AROUND THE BLOCK
The AARF Generation

A FEW MOVES LEFT

---

want a sniff and tumble with a babe who
remembers life before the Macarena and
campaign-finance reform. Looks not important, but if you're a long-legged Ann Margret
type, it's smooch while I still have my teeth.
No Corgis.

COUNTRY FELLER

Down-home farm boy fixin' to come a-
courtin'. If you've ever slept under the stars
with a belly full of s'mores, then you know
what stokes my fire. Sturdy, kind heart, good
morals, and one helluva fox chaser. Lookin' to
lasso a pretty little thing that knows how to
rustle up a possum, likes a bath on Sunday,
and doesn't mind being seen in town with a
square like me.

CLEAN-LIVING DIRTY BLONDE

No-nonsense, empty-nested mother of six
with great teats and teeth seeks meaningless
relationship with a very naughty boy. No
barkers, biters, or stupid pet tricks—been
there, done that. The eye? I'll tell you all
about it over dinner . . . wink, wink.

SINGLE DAD

I have one young son who is my pride and joy.
He fills my life, but there's always room for
more. Legally I'm an adult—but really a kid
at heart. I'm not a Don Johnson but not so
bad too. I get lonely sometimes and wish that
I could have someone to share my thoughts
with. Your interests are mine if I'm interested
in you. Prefer single mom so the priorities are
commonly understood. I would like to hear
from you.

THE SCENT OF TRUE LOVE

Down-to-earth Bloodhound with a nose for
bull. Had a near-death experience when I
choked on a biscuit. Now I'd rather watch the
squirrels than chase them. On the trail of a
new romantic partner is loving, licensed,
and knows how to make a huntin' dog's jowls
drop. If you like the simple life, there's room
for two on my front porch. Bichon Frises? I
reckon not.

WHO'S YOUR DADDY?

I've had enough of old broads trying to teach
me new tricks. Now I want 'em young and
stupid. If you haven't even broken in your
first squeaky toy and don't understand "no"
yet, then maybe we can play. Just be paper
trained.

MULLET UNDER CONSTRUCTION

Recently out lesbian mom looking to get my
feet wet in the waters of Sappho sisterhood. I
enjoy lumberyards, HGTV, sunsets, and anything from Eva Cassidy. You be lipstick, gentle and understanding of an old dog on a new
path. Looking forward to sharing the rainbow
of my orgasm with someone other than
myself. Katie Couric look-alikes a real +

Doublewide King ready to crown my new Queen. Honest-living, honest-loving tow-truck assist wants someone to share the good times with. Got 2 kids that live with their mother in Prescott. Not looking for more. Full-figure girls make me smile. Writing ain't my thing, so if you like what you see and have all your teeth, then hit me up and we'll take it from there.

IT'S NEVER TOO LATE

Long-in-the-tooth Tramp type looking for a Lady to love. Seen the U.S. of A. from the cab of an 18-wheeler. Had the good fortune to pee in 43 different states, with pictures to prove it. New lookin' to put down some roots and pooper-scoop my own backyard. Ready for the picket fence, home-cooked meals and a litter to teach how to play ball. Stable provider — full benefits and enough savings to stake our future. Will you be part of it?

SUPER SENIOR

Former stray seeks soul mate to spend twilight with. Friends first and then . . . ? Cataracts have given me the chance to look inside, and I like what I see. Are you what else I'm looking for? Abusers and neglecters move on. This old-timer's seen it all. Surprise me.

HAVE YOU SEEN MY HEART?

Recently ended a long term relationship or, rather, it ended me. I'm giving love one last try before I bury my heart for good. I don't help the blind cross the street or save children from burning buildings. I'm just a dog asking another dog to love me. Interested? Then start digging.

I'VE GOT ONE LEFT AFTER MY DIVORCE

Recently single and back in circulation. Not bitter — just wiser. A woman with too much time on her hands is bound to stray — especially when your freeloading half-bother lives with you. I've cleaned house (God forbid she ever did) and am ready to move on. Cheating, lying, selfish, controlling studs: Don't bother.

ANYTHING GOES

Dogs Gone Wild

RETIRED LORD AND LADY SEEK WILLING PEASANTS

The children are grown and we're ready to

Naughty infidels, not easy to shock. You: Discreet, not of royal blood, and extremely submissive. Sound like Camelot? Then let's meet at the renaissance fair, and ride the wild serf. Breed? Surprise us.

LIKE JUMPING OUT OF MOVING CARS?

ME TOO!!

ONE LUMP OR TWO?

Territorial Teacup with S&M bent demands submissive playthings for long nights of pleasure and pain. My nails are clipped but not my libido. If you've been a bad, bad boy then I want to hear from you. Are you man enough to be my lapdog? I thought so. Roll over and beg.

YES, LADIES, WE'RE SINGLE

Two fun L.A. brothers (adopted) seek two extraordinary Poodlettes (same litter okay) for indoor/outdoor games. All you need to know is we're bathed, neutered, and very limber. Come live the fairy tail. What happens in Silver Lake, stays in Silver Lake.

I LIKE TO DRESS UP

Plucky mutt who looks great in heels. I've been Marilyn for Halloween, Barbra on my birthday, and Boy George for the hell of it. I'm looking for a sensitive sidekick who shares my love of all things costume. Breed not important, but if you're good with a needle and thread so much the better. No fleas. No queens. No kidding.

I'M NOT AS CRAZY AS I LOOK—I'M CRAZIER

Petite and powerful Natalie Wood type who can swim. Shiny brindle coat, hypnotic eyes, full lips, and a fire down below! No limits party girl who digs a good dig and respects a man who knows how to bury a bone. Let's hook up if you wanna push my envelope and nip at the mailman of passion.

OPEN RELATIONSHIP

She's bi-curious with a taut, hot body that is one raw nerve I can't seem to satisfy alone. I like to share, love to watch, and will let you walk away with all photo negatives. You be tartar free and eager to please. Droolers encouraged. The rest is chemistry.

ON THE LAM FROM ANIMAL CONTROL

Handsome I did hate the DGS man. I can't be the only one who hates that brown uniform. I'm incognito, on the run, and I could sure use a little love and a good meal. If you like bad boys and have a nice nighttime-for-two away from the glaring eye of the law, then maybe you're what I'm looking for. No hang-ups please. I have my own problems.

FOUR LEGS OVER EASY

Gourmet girl with low limits wants men with big appetites and enormous spatulas to flip me over for an all-you-can-eat buffet. Sloppy

floor. First come, first served. If you like it hot and spicy and know your way around the kitchen, then let's get cooking. Seconds anyone?

I'VE BEEN A BAD GIRL

Petite Latina needs a new place to live. They threw me out. Excuse me if I have a small bladder and no impulse control. I can't think romance right now, but once I settle into your place, who knows. Only respond if you don't have nice carpet. I've been through enough. And no Boxers. I'm not that desperate.

DON'T JUDGE WHAT YOU DON'T UNDERSTAND

Mixed couple with no limits and no tolerance for prejudice. We seek other open singles and couples who see past the societal barriers and into the true meaning of love. We host free, bi-monthly swing events at our San Fernando Valley home. Leave your inhibitions at the door. The hot tub is ready — snacks and towels provided. All welcome—single men must be prescreened. Peace.

ROLE-PLAY FANTASIES EXPLORED

Creative, open-minded Beagle invites dominant females for massage, body worship, and bondage games at my private Pasadena doghouse. Let's play Veterinarian, Postman, or Spin the Rawhide. Please be imaginative, verbal, and flexible. I can take a lickin' and give one too. Short-hair breed preferred—but won't discriminate. Your pleasure is my only goal. Mistress.

IGNORE MY WIFE

Sorry you ever shed singlehood? Me too. Need to break free from the choke chain of relentless "companionship" and commitment? Ditto. Sick of the barked orders, the whimpering guilt trips, the honey-do list? I hear you. Enough is finally enough. Let's walk out our doggy doors and into each other's heart. You first.

CHANCE MEETINGS

Waiting to do do do

LONE PINE CAMPGROUND: LAST FOURTH OF JULY

You're black, on the right. We sat behind the same rock and sat out the fireworks. We shared life stories, and more, but no names. Sound familiar? Well, you're a father. You have four daughters and a son who want to meet their daddy. Come home. Yes, of course they're yours.

YOGAWORKS ON MAIN

Iyengar. Last Thursday morning. I complimented the arch on your Downward Facing Dog. You thought my Cat Pose was phoned in. I've recently shed my negative karmic thing-amed experience, forsest chastogess.

RETIRED LORD AND LADY
SEEK WILLING PEASANTS

The children are grown and we're ready to lower the drawbridge and have some medieval fun with a like-minded couple. Us: Naughty infidels, not easy to shock. You: Discreet, not of royal blood, and extremely submissive. Sound like Camelot? Then let's meet at the renaissance fair, and ride the wild serf. Breed? Surprise us.

LIKE JUMPING OUT OF MOVING CARS?
ME TOO!!

ONE LUMP OR TWO?

Territorial Teacup with S&M bent demands submissive playthings for long nights of pleasure and pain. My nails are clipped but not my libido. If you've been a bad, bad boy, then I want to hear from you. Are you man enough to be my lapdog? I thought so. Roll over and beg.

YES, LADIES, WE'RE SINGLE

Two fun L.A. brothers (adopted) seek two extraordinary Poodlettes (same litter okay) for indoor/outdoor games. All you need to know is we're bathed, neutered, and very limber. Come live the fairy tail. What happens in Silver Lake, stays in Silver Lake.

I LIKE TO DRESS UP

Plucky mutt who looks great in heels. I've been Marilyn for Halloween, Barbra on my birthday, and Boy George for the hell of it. I'm looking for a sensitive sidekick who shares my love of all things costume. Breed not important, but if you're good with a needle and thread so much the better. No fleas. No queens. No kidding.

I'M NOT AS CRAZY AS I LOOK–I'M CRAZIER

Petite and powerful Natalie Wood type who can swim. Shiny brindle coat, hypnotic eyes, full lips, and a fire down below! No-limits party girl who digs a good dig and respects a man who knows how to bury a bone. Let's hook up if you wanna push my envelope and nip at the mailman of passion.

OPEN RELATIONSHIP

She's bi-curious with a taut, hot body that is one raw nerve I can't seem to satisfy alone. I like to share, love to watch, and will let you walk away with all photo negatives. You be tartar free and eager to please. Droolers encouraged. The rest is chemistry.

ON THE LAM FROM ANIMAL CONTROL

Maybe I did bite the UPS man. I can't be the only one who hates that brown uniform. I'm incognito, on the run, and I could sure use a little love and a good meal. If you like bad boys and have a nice doghouse-for-two away from the glaring eye of the law, then maybe you're what I'm looking for. No hang-ups please. I have my own problems.

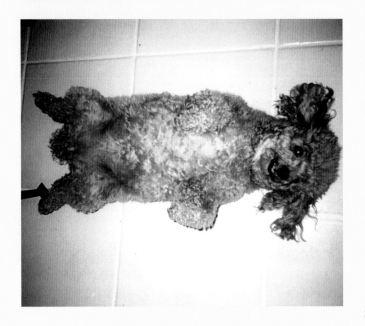

FOUR LEGS OVER EASY

Gourmet girl with few limits wants men with big appetites and enormous spatulas to flip me over for an all-you-can-eat buffet. Sloppy eaters at my house make for a feast on the floor. First come, first served. If you like it hot and spicy and know your way around the kitchen, then let's get cooking. Seconds anyone?

I'VE BEEN A BAD GIRL

Petite Latina needs a new place to live. They threw me out. Excuse me if I have a small bladder and no impulse control. I can't think romance right now, but once I settle into your place, who knows. Only respond if you don't have nice carpet. I've been through enough. And no Boxers. I'm not *that* desperate.

DON'T JUDGE
WHAT YOU DON'T UNDERSTAND

Mixed couple with no limits and no tolerance for prejudice. We seek other open singles and couples who see past the societal barriers and into the true meaning of love. We host free, bi-monthly swing events at our San Fernando Valley home. Leave your inhibitions at the door. The hot tub is ready—snacks and towels provided. All welcome—single men must be prescreened. Peace.

ROLE-PLAY FANTASIES EXPLORED

Creative, open-minded Beagle invites dominant females for massage, body worship, and bondage games at my private Pasadena doghouse. Let's play Veterinarian, Postman, or Spin the Rawhide. Please be imaginative, verbal ,and flexible. I can take a lickin' and give one too. Short-hair breed preferred—but won't discriminate. Your pleasure is my only goal, Mistress.

IGNORE MY WIFE

Sorry you ever shed singlehood? Me too. Need to break free from the choke chain of relentless "companionship" and commitment? Ditto. Sick of the barked orders, the whimpering guilt trips, the honey-do list? I hear you. Enough is finally enough. Let's walk out our doggy doors and into each other's heart. You first.

...Flocky until who looks great in heels. I've been Marilyn for Halloween. Barbra on my birthday, and Boy George for the hell of it. I'm looking for a sensitive sidekick who shares my love of all things costume. Breed not important, but if you're good with a needle and thread so much the better. No fleas. No queens. No kidding.

I'M NOT AS CRAZY AS I LOOK—I'M CRAZIER

Petite and powerful Natalie Wood type who can swim. Shiny brindle coat, hypnotic eyes, full lips, and a fire down below! No-limits party girl who digs a good dig and respects a man who knows how to bury a bone. Let's hook up if you wanna push my envelope and nip at the mailman of passion.

OPEN RELATIONSHIP

She's bi-curious with a taut, hot body that is one raw nerve I can't seem to satisfy alone. I like to share, love to watch, and will let you walk away with all photo negatives. You be tartar free and eager to please. Droolers encouraged. The rest is chemistry.

ON THE LAM FROM ANIMAL CONTROL

Maybe I did bite the UPS man, I can't be the only one who hates that brown uniform. I'm incognito, on the run, and I could sure use a little love and a good meal. If you like bad boys and have a nice doghouse-for-two away from the glaring eye of the law, then maybe you're what I'm looking for. No hang-ups please. I have my own problems.

FOUR LEGS OVER EASY

Gourmet girl with few limits wants men with big appetites and enormous spatulas to flip me over for an all-you-can-eat buffet. Sloppy eaters at my house make for a feast on the floor. First come, first served. If you like it hot and spicy and know your way around the kitchen, then let's get cooking. Seconds anyone?

I'VE BEEN A BAD GIRL

Petite Latina needs a new place to love. They threw me out. Excuse me if I have a small bladder and an impulse control. I can't think romance right now, but once I settle into your place, who knows. Only respond if you don't have nice carpet. I've been through enough. And no Boxers. I'm not *that* desperate.

DON'T JUDGE MY BOOK BY MY TOLERANCE

Mixed couple with no limits and no tolerance for prejudice. We seek other open singles and couples who see past the societal barriers and into the true meaning of love. We host free, bi-monthly swing events at our San Fernando Valley home. Leave your inhibitions at the door. The hot tub is ready---towels and towels provided. All welcome---single men must be prescreened. Peace.

Kennel hostilities on Mississippi. Body wrestling, bondage games at my private Pasadena doghouse. Let's play Veterinarian, Postman, or Spin the Rawhide. Please be imaginative, verbal, and flexible. I can take a lickin' and give one too. Short-hair breed preferred----but won't discriminate. Your pleasure is my only care, Mistress.

IGNORE MY WIFE

Sorry you ever shed singlehood? Me too. Need to break free from the choke chain of relentless "companionship" and commitment? Ditto. Sick of the barked orders, the whimpering guilt trips, the honey-do list? I hear you. Enough is finally enough. Let's walk out our doggy doors and into each other's heart. You first.

CHANCE MEETINGS
Waiting to Go Out

LONE PINE CAMPGROUND, LAST FOURTH OF JULY

You're black, on the right. We hid behind the same rock and sat out the fireworks. We shared life stories, and more, but no names. Sound familiar? Well, you're a father. You have four daughters and a son who want to meet their daddy. Come home. Yes, of course they're yours.

YOGAWORKS ON MAIN

Iyengar. Last Thursday morning. I complimented the arch on your Downward Facing Dog. You thumped my Cat Pose was aligned in. I've recently shed my negative karma (toxic pound experiences, fascist obedience schools) and am finally ready to share my journey. If you tell the vibe too then let's travel together. Namaste.

WHERE ARE YOU?

You were a stray who magically "washed up" on our doorstep. We fed you and nursed you back to health. I endured your insults because I thought we were falling in love. You promised you'd come back and take me away from my evil parents who never let me do anything. It's been two months. Where the @#$%&* are you? I'm going nuts here. No questions asked.

RIVERSIDE DOG PARK

We ran for the same red Frisbee and carried it back together. So began the best days... changes day of my life. We fetched, we...

...we had something. Then you stopped coming. I ran away, trying to find you. Now I'm leashed and lonely, and I can't look at a Frisbee without crying. Come back. Will wait.

DR. CONDELLO'S MANGE CLINIC

We both looked prehistoric and had some good laughs between scratches. I've cleared up great since then, and am having a hard time finding a guy who wants me for more than my great looks. Just wanted to reconnect with someone who seemed to get one. Sure hope you've cleared up too. If not, that's cool. You have nice eyes.

NORTH SHORE ANIMAL SHELTER

We heard you escaped! Remember us, Bro? Before the shelter we all ran like wolves together, free, living out of Dumpsters, a tight pack. Look at us now, Man! We're clean, living in fancy houses, and have an expensive dog walker. Are you back on the street? Call "Sparkles"? It's time to come in from the cold, Dude. Let's get the old posse together and pick through some suburban trash! C'mon, Dawg!

Looking for Mr. Goodbone

EVER BEEN KISSED BY A SCORPIO?

Medium-sized mixed breed eager to love again. New to this but my friends convinced me. Turn-ons: tennis (balls), long walks, and Sausages. Turn-offs: cats, flea treatments, and "no." Kibble and canned-food girl looking for Mr. Right (not Mr. Right Now) who's smart enough to let me win at tug-of-war. Done some modeling, but want someone who can see past my looks. You don't have to be pedigreed, but I like a man who knows when he needs a bath.

FLATULENT AND FUN

Fatty meats, broccoli, certain cheeses. Let's just say they don't go down quietly. If you like a girl who knows good food, and loves nothing more than ripping out a silent-but-deadly one in a crowded room on a hot summer day, then I've got a little message for you: *pfffft*.

I'M SURROUNDED BY FOOLS

Do you hate your friends too? I don't know much, but there's got to be more to life than tugging, rolling around in God-knows-what, and eating rocks (although dirt is decent). If you're tired of innocuous dog park dates and so much sniffing that goes nowhere, then we might be soul mates. Free most afternoons.

MOONDOGGIE, WHERE ARE YOU?

Sun-worshipping beach babe seeks Big Kahuna who loves to suck up the rays and...

LONE PINE CAMPGROUND:
LAST FOURTH OF JULY

You're black, on the right. We hid behind the same rock and sat out the fireworks. We shared life stories, and more, but no names. Sound familiar? Well, you're a father. You have four daughters and a son who want to meet their daddy. Come home. Yes, of course they're yours.

YOGAWORKS ON MAIN

Iyengar. Last Thursday morning. I complimented the arch on your Downward Facing Dog. You thought my Cat Pose was phoned in. I've recently shed my negative karma (toxic pound experiences, fascist obedience schools) and am finally ready to share my journey. If you felt the vibe too then let's travel together. Namaste.

WHERE ARE YOU?

You were a stray who magically "washed up" on our doorstep. We fed you and nursed you back to health. I endured your insults because I thought we were falling in love. You promised you'd come back and take me away from my evil parents who never let me do anything. It's been two months. Where the @#$%&* are you? I'm going nuts here. No questions asked.

RIVERSIDE DOG PARK

We ran for the same red Frisbee and carried it back together. So began the three most glorious days of my life. We fetched, we laughed, we loved. We both liked beef strips and hated the same Pomeranian. I thought we had something. Then you stopped coming. I ran away, trying to find you. Now I'm leashed and lonely, and I can't look at a Frisbee without crying. Come back. I'll wait.

DR. CONDELLO'S MANGE CLINIC

We both looked prehistoric and had some good laughs between scratches. I've cleared up great since then, and am having a hard time finding a guy who wants me for more than my great looks. Just wanted to reconnect with someone who seemed to get me. Sure hope you've cleared up too. If not, that's cool. You have nice eyes.

NORTH SHORE ANIMAL SHELTER

We heard you escaped! Remember us, Bro? Before the shelter we all ran like wolves together, free, living out of Dumpsters, a tight pack. Look at us now, Man! We're clean, living in fancy houses, and have an expensive dog walker. Are you back on the street? Still "Sparkles"? It's time to come in from the cold, Dude. Let's get the old posse together and pick through some choice suburban trash! C'mon, Dawg!

stardom is in my blood. My grandmother and *Johnny Carson* twice with Joan Embry. My mother booked a guest shot on *21 Jump Street.* They say my father did some stunt work on *Baywatch* but I never knew him (long story). I am: gorgeous, scary talented, ambitious, and unstoppable. You are: connected, not threatened, able to chew with your mouth closed. No musicians, actors, or nonguild writers. Producers and directors move to the head of the line.

MALES
Alpha Dogs

PARTY AT MY HOUSE!
Yo! Yo! Yo! What up, senoritas?! The family is gone and the crib is mine! So let's howl at the moon and roll around on the new carpet. Bring your housebroken, fixed friends, and let's get this thing started! All the food you can eat to the one who can get the refrigerator open. Peace out, y'all!

MURRAY THE K-9
Orthodox mensch who's tired of shvitzing over finding the perfect Jewish-American Poodle. Willing to reform my love life for the right family-oriented shiksa with broad, child-

pal. And the Maltese if you are my dream bitch. I'm the dreamboat that your mother wants you to marry—what are you waiting for? This schlemiel is ready to make a deal.

MR. NICE GUY
Old enough to shave, but still a boy at heart. All my women friends say I'm too great a catch to be single. What gives? Good manners and strong values make for lonely Saturday nights. Nice looking (says my mom), polite, and obedient. Is there a girl out there who wants a traditional guy who still believes in ladies first and the magic of a first sniff? Thank you for your consideration.

DISTEMPERAMENTAL, BUT WORTH IT
No more meds, no more shrinks. I say love me, love my Gemini mood swings. One day I'm sniffing the pretty daisies, and the next I'm gnawing on the remote control, wishing it would rain. Needless to say, I'm an excellent kisser. So look me up, but you probably won't. I hate you. I like classical music. How about you?

2 FAST 2 FURRY
Want to ride shotgun as we cruise down the boulevard of true love? Low-riding, street-smart hombre with fuur on the floor seeks fast women for high-octane adventures. Let

single porn. If you know how to check a lipstick and look good in cha-cha pants, then let's give it a test drive.

COCKEYED OPTIMIST
I still believe in love at first sight, sleeping at the foot of the bed, and "heel." I love how I smell after a bath but can't wait to roll in the mud. A nap in the sun, a scratch behind the ear, and an occasional leg hump are what keep me chasing my tail. I think dog shows should be outlawed, cats are for chasing, and doggie day care is for wimps. Let me know if we see eye to eye.

PURE MUSCLE
All-natural bodybuilder who likes to pump it up with other buff muscle dudes is looking to be worshipped by worked-out honies. Very butch—11 pounds of solid muscle—8% body fat—6-pack abs—big guns—trimmed body hair—nice bubble butt. My pic is for real—you should be too. Will be in Tucson for Pride weekend. Show me what you got, boy! Let's party and play!

YOU ARE GETTING SLEEPY . . .
. . . very, very sleepy . . . look deep, deep into my eyes, Miss Sagittarius . . . let go . . . yes . . . do not resist . . . you are mine . . . yes . . . come to me . . . yes . . . bring us a snack . . . that's it . . . that's it . . . sit . . . stay . . . yes . . . good girl.

YOU HAD ME AT ROLL OVER
Top Dog. Tom Cruise look-alike, seeks sassy Penelope Cruz-ish Chihuahua to pull three G's with. If you dig Jerky McGuire, doing Risky Business, and don't think that love is a Mission Impossible, then I'm the Cocktail Wiener dog for you. Do you have what it takes to be my leading lady? Let's jump on the casting couch and find out.

FIVE THINGS I CAN'T LIVE WITHOUT
Broken-in Tennis Balls, Peanut Butter, Public Television, Love, Broken-in Tennis Balls.

GOING MY WAY?
Forward-thinking bon vivant with an eye toward where I've been. Willing to trade my soul for a 9-pack of chicken tenders and a Shiatsu massage. Well traveled, overeducated, lighthearted. Is it true I'm single because I keep looking for a Bond girl in a dive bar? True love and objects in mirror are closer than they appear. I'd rather be at the Hilton in Paris than with Paris Hilton. Life's a trip—pack lightly. Give me a call and start breaking my heart.

KNOCK KNOCK
Funnyman cutup is seriously looking for you. My comedy may be stand-up, but I'll take my love lyin' down. If fart jokes make you howl and you see the upside of short men, then

PHOTO CREDITS